LIFE CHOICES

Life Choices

THE TEACHINGS OF ABORTION

Linda Weber

SENTIENT PUBLICATIONS

First Sentient Publications edition 2011

A paperback original

Cover design by Kim Johansen, Black Dog Design (www.blackdogdesign.com)
Book design by Timm Bryson
Cover art: *Memories*, Stefano Vitale

Library of Congress Cataloging-in-Publication Data
Weber, Linda, 1944-
  Life choices : the teachings of abortion / by Linda Weber. — 1st Sentient Publications ed.
    p. cm.
  Includes bibliographical references.
  ISBN 978-1-59181-174-9
  1. Abortion—Psychological aspects. 2. Abortion—Moral and ethical aspects. 3. Abortion—Religious aspects. I. Title.
  HQ767.W37 2011
  362.19'8880019—dc22
                    2010043741

Printed in the United States of America
10 9 8 7 6 5 4 3 2 1

SENTIENT PUBLICATIONS
A Limited Liability Company
1113 Spruce Street
Boulder, CO 80302
www.sentientpublications.com

For my children and their children and theirs...

CONTENTS

GRATITUDE PAGES

Life Choices has been long in its birthing. Written over the course of different periods of my life and with much iteration, the book has been touched by countless dear people. No doubt there are some who have slipped from my memory. My apologies if I have failed to include them here.

I owe a deep debt of gratitude to my patients and clients, from whom I learned most of what I know about the healing of abortion issues. A special thanks to those of them who gave permission to include their stories in the book. Care has been taken to change identifying characteristics out of respect for their privacy.

Thank you to Susan Rennie and the instructors from Vermont College of Norwich University for their support and guidance in the creation of my master's thesis, *Healing the Pain of Abortion* (1990, unpublished), which formed the initial core of this book.

Thank you to the Boulder Valley Women's Health Center, then and now, for extraordinary service to the community and for supporting me in my work.

Many people have been instrumental in the creation of this book. It would not be what it is without the deft editing and wise counsel of Connie Shaw, my publisher at Sentient. I am grateful to Hal Zina Bennett, for his immediate grasp of the import of this book, his sage advice about the writer's path, and his friendship. I was privileged to know David

LaChapelle, a bright light and extraordinary teacher, for twenty-five years before his untimely passing in 2009. I am sustained by his insight into the world of soul and his remarkable healing gift. I am grateful to Steven Foster and Meredith Little for the teachings of The Four Shields, an earth-based model of human psychology that reveals our body-mind-soul-spirit nature.

Lisa Ray Turner did a skillful and instructive job of editing an earlier version of the manuscript. Helpful input also came from friends, including Johannah F., Lisa O., Jackie S., and Carl S., Charlotte T., and from my sister, Sara Weber, and my father, John Weber. Lee Cook, Susan Edwards, and Fatu Judy Henderson each offered fascinating and important information about soul. Sue Herner, literary agent, gave me valuable input during the brief time we worked together.

I am grateful to the women of my meditation group for their grounding and devotion to the depths of spiritual life. Also, to the women of my music circle for the beauty and power of the music. I am blessed with circles among circles of women in community and my dear friends and colleagues who keep me anchored and connected.

My daughters, Jennifer and Anne, personify the hopes and dreams of our family. They taught me the depth and power of mother love. Their way of walking in the world inspires me beyond words. My life partner, Emily, has cheerfully lived with the ups and downs of writing this book. I would not be where I am without her intrinsic wisdom about the creative process, her love, and the life we have together.

I salute my ancestors for their love of life, their courage, creativity and intelligence, their desire to live better, and their humor and generosity. A deep bow to my mother and father for the wisdom of their critique of the world's woes and their vision for a better world.

This book would not be possible without the worldwide movement for women's liberation. Boundless gratitude goes to all who struggle around the globe. And lest I forget where I am, a deep bow to Mother Earth and Father Sky and to The Spirit That Moves In All Beings And Things.

INTRODUCTION

It is 1970 in New York City. The laws are changing and it is no longer illegal to have an abortion. Clinics open almost immediately to provide services. I begin counseling in one of those clinics a few months after legalization. Women come for abortions from every part of the United States. Each of them is referred to the clinic by a local clergyman where they live. Some of the women travel long distances; some are young, some older; some are married, most are not; some come with a partner or a friend; many come alone. The women come with stories of their lives. They share them with us. Each story I hear gives me pause to think. As I listen, an underground, hidden aspect of women's lives rises to the surface of my understanding. I am fascinated and drawn in like a wave to the shore.

Something important is happening.

In 1970, little was known about the psychology and spirituality of abortion. The word *abortion* was rarely spoken, its illicit reputation having followed it into the legalized light of day. The subject was shadowy, and the feelings, thoughts, and personal circumstances of the people involved were shrouded in ignorance and mystery. The medical techniques of abortion procedures had not yet been perfected, since most had been used only in clandestine, illegal operations. Most of the highly trained obstetrician-gynecologists who came to work at the New York clinic had to be retrained to do first trimester vacuum aspiration abortion procedures. The first medical director of the clinic had been a reputable, though illegal, abortionist in another state. He had perfected a safe outpatient procedure, which he taught to the other physicians. Within its first year of operation, the clinic was bought by a prominent ob-gyn who changed its name to the Center for Reproductive and Sexual Health (CRASH).

Those of us who accompanied women through their abortions were not called counselors at first. We were trained as medical assistants to the physicians. Our job was to organize the medical supplies for abortion, tell each woman what was going to happen to her, and prepare her for the medical procedure. Then the doctor would come in and perform the abortion, which was completed within fifteen minutes.

We noticed right away that most of the women who came to us as patients needed more than that. They needed to talk about what they were going through and how they felt emotionally. They needed to talk about their fears, their families, and their relationships. Many of the women wondered about their relationship with God. They needed reassurance that they were making the best decision they could.

And, we needed to listen. Most of us were part of the burgeoning women's liberation movement. Women's stories were at the center of our lives. Whatever a woman had to say about her life was interesting to us. We believed that we could "raise the consciousness" of women by encouraging them to tell their stories, and that it was healing for them to open up about their lives. We had been doing that ourselves, meeting in small groups— consciousness raising groups—to bare our hearts about our most intimate concerns about being women.

The women who came as patients to the abortion clinic were from all over the country and from all walks of life. We wanted to help them understand what they were feeling and to know that their feelings were good, normal, natural, and acceptable. Most of us had no formal training in psychology. Our willingness to listen and be supportive came from our politics and our personal experience. Later on down the road, many of us became professional counselors, but that's not the way it started. We invented ourselves through necessity, and created abortion counseling, a combination of medical and psychological counseling that gives women a chance to review their pregnancy decisions and explore their thoughts and feelings about having an abortion.

When I left New York I had counseled upwards of 1,200 women and accompanied them through their abortion procedures. I moved with my two young daughters to the mountains near Boulder, Colorado, and began to take stock of what I had been through. With some extended time for reflection, I could begin to face the flood of personal feelings and questions I had about the powerful nature of abortion. My devotion to women's causes was deepening, and I needed to know more. I needed to understand why abortion was full of swirling energy, why it touched people at their core, why it changed people's lives. The underground river of women's reproductive experiences that surfaced with legalized abortion sometimes raged over rough waters. The endless flow of stories was a torrent of unknown proportions. What was happening here? I needed to know.

In 1973, the United States Supreme Court ruled, in the now well known Roe v. Wade decision, that women could freely obtain abortions legally as long as certain basic stipulations were met. In the middle of that year, I joined with a small group of women and men to create the Boulder Valley Clinic, which became Boulder Valley Women's Health Center and is now called Women's Health. It is the first freestanding abortion clinic in the state. We opened for services on the first of November of that year. I worked there for fourteen years.

I've been gathering my thoughts and organizing my questions since those early years. I've been exploring philosophical and spiritual truths and doing what I can to gain understanding about the relationship of abortion to the rest of Life and what it has to teach us. The result is this book, which I offer to you now. It is written primarily for women, but is also for anyone who has an interest and concern about the direction in which the world is headed and about the quality of our relationship with the Earth.

The feminist urge to bring women's issues to the forefront of human life has been a principal motivator for me. At the same time, spiritual concepts that reveal the interrelationship of All Life beg to be seen as the basis for understanding the place of major issues like abortion in the life of society. The essentially pro-life nature of abortion and its spiritual teachings will help us learn to integrate different levels of consciousness about Life. This book addresses many levels of the abortion issue, including the personal, the political and historical, the psychological, and the spiritual.

The perspective I am bringing through is large and inclusive. It shows how reality dances between the personal and the collective and between nature and culture. My intention is to make it easier for us to see our daily lives and personal issues in the context of our ongoing planetary evolution. It is challenging to try to capture the patterns of the dance on paper. One way I do this is to capitalize *Life* when it means the same thing as *All Life*. *Nature, Earth* and *Spirit* are also often capitalized. Using language this way allows me to bring attention to the spiritual importance of these concepts.

When an all-inclusive framework is added to the abortion debate, functional political categories like *pro-choice* and *pro-life* start to dissolve. This is natural, but there is a danger in it. It would be worse than foolish to set aside the struggle to keep abortion safe and legal simply because we want to challenge simplistic slogans.

I believe abortion is essentially pro-life, because my experience has shown me how it can enrich women's lives. Large numbers of women could not have succeeded as lawyers and doctors, scientists and engineers, without the availability of abortion. Women have a greater degree and sense of safety in their lives because they know they can control the number of children born from their bodies without risk to themselves. The changes we have seen in the status of women in the last forty years in this country would not have been possible without significant numbers of women being able to obtain abortions when they needed them.

I see Life in a simultaneously timeless and time-bound way. It operates in the spiritual place of soul and in the physical, time-based dimension in which we live our daily lives. While we explore spiritual and philosophical realms, we remain committed to the improvement of life in the physical realm, the relative world in which we move through our days. Legal, freely chosen abortion is an enormous stepping-stone to authentic empowerment and autonomy for women. Our commitment to women's health needs, one of which is the availability of safe abortion, must stay strong while we argue thorny issues and concerns. Anyone who is realistic about the slow progress of consciousness about sex, and the economic instability in which most people live their relationships, will conclude that we must keep abortion legal if we are to move forward in our lives. It would be immoral to do otherwise. History and society give us no choice but to be "pro-choice." We are not free if we do not have reproductive freedom.

I find it curious that some in the pro-choice movement have bought into the propaganda of the pro-life movement, and have become defensive about abortion. I've heard, from people who should know better, that "no one *wants* an abortion." While it's true that until we need one we don't aspire to have one, women who are pregnant and who feel strongly that they don't want to be pregnant *want* abortions. Need and want merge in the unwanted pregnancy situation. There is no difference between them. We shouldn't be apologetic about wanting women to be able to have abortions when they want them.

Those of us who make specific choices about life exercise responsibility for Life. Conscious decisions about pregnancy bring us into direct contact with primal cycles of Nature and our own nature. Cycles, by their very nature, can upset our equilibrium and put us in a state of chaos because they are full of transitions and changing conditions. Pregnancy decision making is more basic than beautiful, more like a mudslide than a meadow. When we make decisions to bring pregnancy forward or to turn it back we merge our basic intuitive instincts with our ability to reason, but it's easy to feel stuck in the heaviness of conflicting pressures.

The current psychology of abortion is rooted in historical realities and in the pernicious alienation of our culture from the natural world. Consequently, we are estranged from our own bodies. Sometimes we think we are separate from our bodies, that we can manipulate them, as we would some machine outside of ourselves. A pregnancy crisis can explode these untruths and rearrange our thinking to the core.

Death and Birth conspire together in abortion. Their unity defies conventional perception. It makes us rethink our ideas about Life. I have sat with many hundreds of women as they unraveled the tangled web of misunderstanding that confounded their hearts and minds. They were in touch, often unknowingly, with a deep stream of female experience. This historical and spiritual stream contains the millions of women who came before. They and we embody the regenerative power of the Earth.

Life on Earth is full of life-death-life cycles. What is our place in all that? How does our consciousness fit with that? As women, how can we achieve greater autonomy, while at the same time serve our legacy of relationship? How can we be sure that the freedom we seek is consonant with the love in our lives? Can we learn to care for others and ourselves without sacrificing ourselves? Can we reduce our suffering without destroying that which is closest to our hearts? What does it mean to live from power?

Most of what I now know about women's experiences with abortion I learned from the women for whom I was a counselor. Some of these women were in groups; most were individual clients. Women who have come to me for psychotherapy have shown me the depth of perspective that can be obtained by exploring private fears and vulnerabilities over time. All of them displayed uncommon moral courage by opening their hearts and minds to self-examination.

The Women's Liberation Movement has sustained my hope for a better world. I salute those feminists who have stuck with it, stayed on track, forged new paths, and broken new ground. When I began counseling in abortion clinics there were no safehouses, no rape crisis centers, nowhere for battered or assaulted women to go for shelter or care. Belief was widespread that if a woman was hurt by a man "she had it coming," she must have "done something" to provoke the assault. Worse, if she was married, her husband's violent behavior was excused as natural, even normal. After all, she was *his*. Jokes about "wife beating" were common. If a woman became pregnant "out of wedlock," her status in the eyes of society automatically dropped. Married women were expected to have all babies they were impregnated with. Single women were expected to be chaste. Heterosexuality was assumed. No one spoke of any other way to be. For millions of women around the world, it is still this way.

The widespread use of birth control methods had not permeated society yet. Anything related to sex and sexuality was hush-hush, taboo, off limits, not to be talked about openly, and in some places illegal. "Living in sin" was a popular phrase to describe an unmarried woman and man who lived together. More likely than not, an unmarried couple would have to fake marriage in order to rent an apartment or stay in a hotel together. "Shotgun" marriages were commonplace.

No universities had women's studies departments and many of the most prestigious schools did not admit women at all. Organized sports programs for women were rare and never required. There were no sexual harassment laws. Women earned half as much as men for the same work. (This has improved only a little.) The word *sexism* was just being born in popular language. *Mankind* described humans of both sexes. Male pronouns were used to make universal statements and included female people, or so it was claimed.

Today, there has been some movement towards meaningful change in the quality of women's lives. Women have more legal protection on the job and more choices in employment. Male supremacy is no longer assumed to be the natural way in all circumstances. In many quarters, sex is more openly discussed and both women and men feel freer to admit their vulnerabilities and needs. The use of birth control is widely recognized as a good idea for sexually active people, married or not. AIDS has brought a new understanding of the need to be vigilant and self-protective. Legal abortion has made it clear that women are determined to control reproduction and the direction of our lives.

But these and other changes, while encouraging and good, are just the beginning, and they are precarious and uneven. There are too many people, women as well as men, who are still afraid of full equality for women. Narrow religious concepts still have great influence over the minds and hearts of people. The feminist movement and the magnitude of the changes it advocates regarding self-definition and family roles continue to be regarded with suspicion. Most of all, the fabric of society is still dominated by patterns of exploitation, both economic and cultural, that limit the ability of most people to be secure that their basic needs will be met.

Most people in the United States depend upon the whims of large corporations for jobs that often don't pay enough to live comfortably and could suddenly disappear if their company finds a cheaper source of labor in another town or country. Adequate housing and health care are increasingly less easy to come by for a growing number of people. Our society views its members as consumers rather than as citizens and creative beings. We are encouraged to sell ourselves to get jobs, almost as if we were products rather than people, just to make enough money to survive.

The sea of exploitation in which we all swim is bolstered by fear—that we won't "make it," that we are powerless to take charge of our lives, that we are "not good enough." This is especially true for women, because centuries of subordination have installed in us an ingrained, shared inferiority complex. Freely chosen abortion challenges this because it asks each woman who considers it to step into her personal power and take charge of her life. It asks us as a society to recognize that the act of saying no to unwelcome intrusions is courageous and good.

By revealing the teachings of abortion, I hope to give vision to what needs to be done to assure a better life for all people.

The spiritual perspective I put forward here is one I've gained by spending a great deal of time in the wilderness of the Colorado mountains. Befriending and opening to more-than-human Nature has been my way to heal my own imbalances and understand the interconnectedness of All Life. My spiritual perspective begins and ends with Spirit in Nature.

A few years ago I went on a personal, contemplative retreat to meditate on the writing of this book. The setting was an abbey on a portion of mountainous land in northern Colorado.

On my drive to the abbey from Boulder, a large bird of prey appears in the sky overhead and flies ahead of my car for a few miles. On the third day of my retreat, I am swept up by a compelling urge to climb as high as possible. The energy pushes me intuitively to go higher, to place myself above everything else, to get to the highest point on the land and then to look down and out to see all that I can see.

Climbing steadily up the mountainside, I pray for perspective, for deeper vision, for a point of view that takes in the whole picture and sees from a higher place. I want to write the book from that perspective, in a way that makes sense to people. The edge of the steep rock hillside overlooks a small canyon that drops hundreds of feet into a roaring creek below, water that had cut through the canyon for eons. Here is Earth, showing itself to me in slow geologic time, history in layers of rock. A higher, deeper perspective on abortion is indeed possible, according to the guidance I am receiving from the land. The many layers of the issue will be revealed if I find the right vantage point and learn to see with the eyes of an eagle.

Nature shows us in no uncertain terms that Life is a never-ending flow of experiences. Some of these are pleasant and easy, like a sunny summer day, and some are turbulent and frightening, like a sudden avalanche on a seemingly serene mountain. Some are significant while others are not. All are valid and legitimate. Abortion shows us the underbelly of Nature, like the decomposing rot of a fallen tree covering rich, dark soil. It is a compelling experience that directs us to be in alignment with our true nature and the cycles of our lives. Abortion is inherently moral when we see it in the context of our responsibility to Life.

As history moves and Life evolves we are pressed to expand our awareness. Facing issues of life, death, and rebirth, intrinsic to the abortion experience, mandates us to adopt an attitude towards Life that recognizes death and change as legitimate and even good. This perspective is one that takes life and death seriously. It maintains a respectful and vigilant attitude towards the flow of life energies. It balances freedom and responsibility in our life choices.

Inside personal pain is power. Inside the pain of abortion is knowledge about death and rebirth, about change, about relationships, about Life.

When we put our knowledge and power together, we grow in ways that are true to our essential nature.

Take a moment. Close your eyes and see the whole Earth with your inner eye. Ask yourself for a higher perspective—one that is not bogged down in narrow concerns, but that shows you the *All* of Life and the Soul of Humanity. Ask yourself to be open-minded, to be willing to look at human events with curiosity and compassion. Try to look at abortion that way.

The Spirit of Abortion

What does it mean to accept spiritual responsibility in our lives? How can we be still enough or clear enough or compassionate enough to let the deep truth emerge?

—SHERRY RUTH ANDERSON & PATRICIA HOPKINS,
THE FEMININE FACE OF GOD

TALI SAT ON THE OTHER SIDE OF THE WAITING ROOM IN THE bright daylight of a nearby window. I walked towards her and smiled. "Hi, I'm Linda," I said. "I'm going to be your counselor today. Let's go upstairs." She rose and followed me up the comfortably carpeted stairs of the old house our staff had converted into a women's clinic. We entered one of the cozy counseling rooms, the size of a walk-in closet, and settled into the simple, tan, upholstered armchairs, facing about three feet across from each other. A diminutive end table to the side of our chairs completed the furnishings. On it was a plastic model of the female reproductive system and the paraphernalia of surgical and contraceptive props and educational handouts that would help me explain reproductive anatomy, pregnancy, birth control, and abortion.

The initial form she filled out when she arrived for her appointment asked her how she felt about having an abortion. This is what she wrote:

For me, abortion is like pinching the leaves off the mother plant to let it grow.

Her words took my breath away. They resonate still. Her spirit-filled, poetic insight captures the essence of abortion, its innate creativity, and its underlying life-enriching dimension. It reveals hidden aspects of the experience of abortion. It offers a perspective that digs below surface conflicts to display a deeper truth, for it allows us to see how the act of abortion is part of the Web of Life, the connectedness that, like a rhizome, binds us all.

Pinching leaves, the intentional killing of some of the new growth of a plant, is an act that nurtures and strengthens the plant as a whole. The buds that are pinched and the timing of the act of pinching contribute significantly to the direction of growth and to the final shape of the parent plant. Tali's simple metaphor suggests that the way to understand and heal conflicts about abortion is to look to the natural world, and understand that our lives are part of an intricate pattern of interdependent relationships that make up all of Life.

Tali's decision to have an abortion was made mindfully. She was clear that it was in her own best interest. She believed that the bud of her pregnancy should not progress any further, so she ended the pregnancy. Tali believed her body was like the bodies of other animals and plants in Nature. Few of us think of ourselves that way. Most women are pained about having an abortion. They are caught up in a storm of emotions and conflicts and are scared and unhappy. Tali showed me that another way is possible. She inspired me to develop a holistic understanding of abortion, and to perceive the pain of abortion in light of what it can teach us.

A Holistic Perspective

Tali saw her pregnancy and herself as parts of social and spiritual ecosystems—living entities operating within living entities, like trees in a forest. This is a truly novel way to grasp the complexity of the interdependent environment in which we make choices about pregnancy. Tali's goal was to preserve the equilibrium of her personal ecosystem—the body-mind-soul-spirit of her being—in order to have a say in defining the terms of her relationships and the direction of her life.

A tree that drops its seed too close to itself will not see that seed flower. The ground will not support it. The forest will nurture the offspring of one of its trees only when the placement of a seedling serves the forest as a whole. It's hard to think of the death of a seedling in a forest as a death at all. It seems more like a cooperative surrender to the greater whole.

Of course, human consciousness is different from plant consciousness. We are aware—of the world around us, our history, and ourselves. We experience our relationships in uniquely human ways. We treasure them. We have ambivalence and grief about them. We have free will, reason, and choice. We have trouble letting go. More than anything, we want to make the right choices in our lives.

Abortion is a collection of some of the most difficult issues related to human growth and development, both individual and societal. One of these is the struggle of women for freedom and autonomy in the context of the patriarchal paradigm—that ocean of living history in which we all swim—where men and the male way is dominant and women and the female way is subordinate. The avenues open to women have been littered with limitations imposed on us by laws and customs that authorize our inferiority. One of the most fundamental of these is the expectation that having children is more important for us than anything else, and that we will subordinate ourselves to make that happen.

The intensely personal spiritual and psychological task of self-development is also an historical task, as personal life always takes place in the context of human history and the life of the planet. Nothing that happens to us personally happens in a vacuum. It is always surrounded and contained by larger social and spiritual realities.

Permission to have choices in pregnancy, especially the choice of abortion, suggests that we have to change the way we are in our most intimate relationships. We have to become proactive, assertive, clear about our own needs, and willing to take the lead in relation to how things go.

This is not easy and can be scary. Yes, we want to flower as individuals, but not without our most cherished relationships! Yet, some relationships stand in the way of our best chance to grow into ourselves, and we find ourselves pinching the leaves off our mother plant selves. Underlying the many valid reasons for having an abortion—reasons prompted by necessity and life circumstances—is the pulsing of a new way of being in our lives, a way based on self-respect, autonomy, safety, and equality.

The part of us that has agreed, even tacitly, to be subordinate has to die in order to make this possible. But this self-sabotaging part does not die easily. It tries to convince us that we *need* to be dependent, that we do not and should not have the power to freely create, and that we should sacrifice ourselves to limited ways of living. The main way women have done this is by having children we don't want to have. That we typically learn to love these children in spite of ourselves makes this no less true.

A holistic perspective on abortion recognizes that abortion is a gateway for women and men to learn to make conscious, life-enhancing choices, and to gain awareness about the nature of Life. Abortion as a considered choice asks that we adopt a strong commitment to our own freedom and throw off history's beast of burden yoke. This is true whether the decision is to have an abortion or to go ahead with a pregnancy and have a child. The clash of opposing expectations, feelings, and obligations in the consideration of abortion pushes people to gather their strength and claim their personal power, like a giant wave in a rising tide.

Wholeness

Wholeness is a natural state of balance that encompasses constantly shifting patterns of living and perceiving. It is achieved by becoming conscious about all aspects of self. The road to psychological wholeness is paved with difficult experiences that challenge our ability to be active in our own interest, as well as our ability to understand how our lives connect to the lives of others. Wholeness includes all aspects of our lives: physical, psychological, mental, and spiritual, "good" and "bad." It embraces all levels of experience—personal, collective, and universal.

Just as trees follow their natural pathways towards growth, so, too, do human beings. As we live our lives, events occur that give us opportunities to gain the awareness we need to become whole. When a life experience comes along like a big wind and sweeps us into its embrace, we are forced to surrender to its power and allow it to toss us around until we land on our feet. When the experience comes from the shadow side of life, it provokes fear and a sense of a descent into darkness. Abortion is often this kind of experience.

The shadow is that which is not in the light. It is part of Nature, like night and things associated with night, or being underground. Our collective fear of the dark has made what dwells there problematic for us. Instead of welcoming the mystery of the night, we try to light it away. For example, our cities are now emitting so much artificial light at night that many of us are suffering from sleep disorders caused by light pollution. Our lives are out of balance because we try to drive away the darkness.

The psychological shadow is full of unconsciously disowned parts of us that have been pushed away to meet the expectations of our families, churches, and schools. It contains a compost of possibilities for the growth of wholeness. For example, if I have squirreled away my ability to say no when a friend or family member asks me to do what they want, the perception of myself as powerless, and the gnawing feeling of being controlled by someone or something else will haunt my daily life. If I become pregnant at a rough time of my life and turn towards considering abortion, I will be forced to face my inability to assert my own needs and opinions. My autonomous self will be pressed to step out of the shadow.

The natural quest for wholeness invites experiences that will rectify imbalances and give us knowledge and comfort about the power of aspects of our lives that have been pushed out of our awareness. Sex and death, two of the most essential aspects of abortion, reside in the shadow of modern life as well as in our personal psychic shadows. Life events that have their source in sex and death are profoundly transformational.

Right Relationship

The inner experience of conflict around a pregnancy often revolves around perceptions of relationship. Women generally tend to be focused on relationships. A pregnancy that leads to abortion often leads us into a close examination of how we are living our relationships, both personally and in the larger scheme of things. A common example of this is the tendency among women to "shrink to fit," i.e., make ourselves smaller and less significant in relation to men. Facing her options in pregnancy can make a woman question this behavior.

The urge to live in a balanced way is natural for all individual life forms and for the life of the Earth as a whole. Earth organizes Life around right relationship and the interrelationship of all beings and things. The balanced state of being in Life is a state of right relationship and is necessary for wholeness.

The urge to be in right relationship usually governs a woman's process of choosing abortion, even if she is not consciously aware of it at the time. She will feel sure that having a baby at an inopportune time in her life is wrong. She will express concern for the welfare of her potential child if she is not able to relate to it in a nurturing way. Self-examination in terms of right relationship can change the course of a person's life.

Right relationship is a cultural concept that can be found in the beliefs and practices of indigenous peoples around the world. It is helpful to remember that the heritage of all peoples is originally indigenous. Every human on the planet is descended from other humans whose ancestors were native to a landed place. Even now there is no avoiding the fact that each of us is indigenous to planet Earth in spite of the fact that we might feel disconnected from the land on which our lives depend.

The idea of right relationship leads naturally towards a morality that is centered in individual and collective existence, rather than individual rights. This morality is about the existence of individuals in right relationship with other individuals and with the environment. The whole and parts of the whole are seen together. They are never separated. It emphasizes the importance of context in assessing individual behavior and need. The movement towards sustainable communities incorporates this kind of morality. So does public health policy that puts the needs of people in a compassionate framework.

A morality of right relationship allows forms of life to come into being and pass away without judgment and without valuing one form over another. It requires strong powers of observation and a willingness to be objective in matters that are intimately subjective. It also requires a sense of compassionate responsibility to oneself and one's relationships. To be in Life this way one is asked to take an active part in one's destiny and to develop the skills of responsible choice.

Responsible Choice

Responsible choice emerges when we recognize the direction of our development and move in ways that are consonant and harmonious with the realities in which we live. When we exercise responsible choice in pregnancy we determine whether to bring life through our bodies. This plays itself out as one woman chooses to have a baby and another woman chooses to have an abortion. Each woman's perception of her life circumstances is her own. Our sense of relationship to a pregnancy is part of our sense of relationship to all the elements of our environment.

Conscious Creation

When pregnancy choice-making is a conscious process, a woman is likely to come to grips with emotionally painful aspects of her life. If it is unconscious, as is often the case, a woman can feel unsafe, threatened, and overwhelmed.

Individual identity and development—the process of wholeness—is completely dependent on interactions with others and with historical forces that contribute to what is possible and likely at a certain point in time.

Identity is also formed by awareness of the spiritual reality of timelessness and how that connects us to all that has gone before, all that is, and all that ever will be. When we become consciously involved in our own development, we are faced with making life-determining choices.

This is easier said than done. Many of us find it so difficult to face ourselves that we engage in self-destructive behavior that prevents us from becoming self-aware. Avoidance of the call to consciousness can take the form of alcohol and drug abuse, or obsession with another person or with work. But Life will continue to throw complicated experiences our way that if deeply examined, can provide us with knowledge that holds keys to our creative selves.

Abortion is this kind of experience for many people.

In the chapters that follow, I show how a crisis pregnancy that ends in abortion can catapult a person into learning to make conscious, life-serving, self-enhancing choices. Within the context of a morality of right relationship, responsible choice strengthens a sense of wholeness.

As we play out our life course in the context of different events that link us to one another, and that are themselves linked, we gain respect for our integrity. This newfound self-respect is the key to being able to develop the ability to consciously create.

The purpose of pregnancy is creation. Its meaningfulness is unquestioned in our culture, for without it no one would exist. However, because women and all things female have been devalued in the last five thousand or so years, pregnancy as a positive expression of female power has been distorted. Instead of reverence and respect for women, in whose bodies pregnancy takes place, society has relegated women to subordinate positions where duty and service to men have taken precedence.

This is changing. Controversy and conflict about abortion in the body politic and in the lives of women is indicative of the natural historical push to rectify centuries old inequalities and omissions in the fabric of human life. Human evolution is moving towards organizing human life around the concept of conscious creation.

This has never happened before.

Up to now, human societies have based their organization on economic necessity. Societies struggle with economic realities that contain brutal polarizations of wealth and poverty. The majority of the world's people struggle just to stay alive, while a minority enjoys the fruits of capitalist production and accumulation.

As slow and heavily mudded as it is, the world economy is lifting out of patterns of oppression and exploitation, and moving in the direction of providing peace and plenty for all people. The presence of legal abortion in this process is freeing up the energy of the world's women to play a more active role in the change.

As world economic development reaches a point of abundance, it will become possible to shift the focus to live in terms of creativity and relationships. Competition will necessarily give way to cooperation, and equality will replace the crushing discrepancies in wealth and opportunity. The tension of world crises around issues such as hunger, diminishing resources, and environmental degradation is paving the way for this monumental shift of life on Earth.

Tension in the area of human reproduction often coalesces around the issue of abortion. Abortion is a source of conflict in most countries and in most major religions, as well as in the hearts and minds of individual women and men. The resolution of this conflict is key to becoming consciously creative, because abortion brings to light the need to be conscious about sexuality, the life-giving energy of creation. Sexuality is expressed through pregnancy as well as through choices about relationships and the direction of our lives. It powers the human family.

Physical creation—sex and pregnancy—has been considered throughout history to be "natural." Being natural—close to Nature—has been associated with women. It has also been associated with being unconscious.

The process of resolving a crisis pregnancy challenges the idea that being natural means being unconscious. Making mindless decisions about pregnancy is becoming a thing of the past.

When we consider abortion, we bring conscious awareness to the natural physical process of creating life. A pregnancy is an organic part of a woman's body. When it becomes part of a conscious process, who she is as an integral person becomes as central as the physical changes in her body. The focus shifts towards a holistic body-mind-soul-spirit perspective, rather than an exclusively physical one. As we confront the possibility of death in pregnancy, we face possible changes in ourselves. These changes have the potential to reorder our entire sense of self. We transform, from passive vessel containing pregnancy to active creators of our own lives.

However, due to the nature of our cultural institutions, a woman may not feel comfortable with being an active creator of her own life. She might not be comfortable with her body, her sexuality, or herself, and might resist the expansion of awareness and creative power that can come from the abortion experience. She could realize that something important is happening for her, but not realize how profound it is. If this is the case, and she tries to return to her previous way of living, she is likely to continue to feel disturbed and unresolved about having had an abortion.

Conscious creation is birthing itself in the human community. The emergence of intentional ways of being is a necessary part of the evolution of life on Earth. What more powerful metaphor could there be for this than the process of making choices about pregnancy? The presence of abortion as a social and personal issue is provoking people to examine themselves and their societies. It raises fundamental issues of life and death, freedom and justice, equality and selfhood, sex and sexuality, family, and the nature of creativity.

If the act of abortion—the pinching of the leaves—is perceived only as a wounding, we blind ourselves to understanding the full nature of the experience. The process deserves more consideration than that and so do we.

Both personal and global healing requires a consciousness that takes all aspects of life into consideration as the world reorganizes itself. To help move this along we must learn the larger meaning of abortion both as a social issue and as a personal experience. Then we as a global community can move beyond abortion to the conscious, creative living of our lives.

My Mother, Myself

My mother was eighteen when she had an abortion. That was in 1930. She told me about it in 1960 when I was sixteen. Her abortion was illegal. She almost bled to death.

I watched her eyes grow wide and fill with tears as she told her story. She breathed deliberately, her chest rising and falling with a heaviness that was incomprehensible to me. There didn't seem to be enough air in the room in which we sat. She described her wrenchingly lonely state of isolation, her fear that she would bleed to death, and how she had been ambushed by strong feelings of loss that she had not known were possible. She remembered an older woman friend of hers who had found her lying on the kitchen floor after the abortion. The woman took my mother to the hospital and saved her life.

What impressed me about my mother's story was her clear, ever-present emotion, as though her abortion had happened yesterday rather than thirty years before. Her emotional honesty and willingness to be open was a great lesson for me about what it is to be human. It was my first glimpse of a woman's reproductive pain, and it laid the basis for my understanding of how to heal that pain.

Three years after hearing my mother's story, I became pregnant and had an abortion. I was nineteen and attending college in the early 1960s in New York City. Though I used a method of birth control most of the time, I wasn't using any at the time I became pregnant. To this day, I don't know why I took that chance.

Almost right away I had a strong sense that I was pregnant. When I missed my period a low level of panic set in. It wasn't legal to obtain an abortion at that time, and it wasn't okay to speak freely about it either. The word *abortion* was taboo.

Neither my boyfriend nor I had any idea what to do. We consulted an older friend who suggested I get a pregnancy test. I remember going to the Margaret Sanger Clinic in New York to get the test. Mostly what I remember is the agony of sitting by the phone in someone's apartment while I waited for the result. It was a nightmare.

When the call came and the voice on the other end said the test was positive, I felt confused. Positive. That means it's the way you want it to be, right? But no, positive meant pregnant, and that's not what I wanted. My skin felt clammy. My head was spinning. Everything felt like it was going much too fast. I was terribly frightened.

For a split second I thought about having the baby. As I thought about it I became more and more clear that having a baby at that time was the last thing in the world I wanted. Actually I wasn't thinking in the usual sense. I was *bodythinking*—behaving as a whole organism. Bodythinking is a natural, nonjudgmental merge of body and mind. Thoughts and behavior fuse into an intuitive stream of action on our own or another's behalf. It is the way we often respond to compelling, unexpected life events.

Over the next several weeks I found myself seeking a way to end the pregnancy. I knew in the deepest place in my heart that having a baby would be the wrong thing for me to do. Seeking an end to that pregnancy was the most natural thing in the world for me. It was something my body and mind, acting as one, told me to do.

My friend's sister gave me the name of a woman to go and talk to about an abortion. It was eerie, the strangeness and peculiar terror of sneaking around. The woman gave me two options. She said that she could try to "do something" to me, or that I could go to the outpatient clinic of a large hospital and request that they insert an intra-uterine device, without telling them that I was pregnant, of course. She said having an IUD inside my uterus would induce an abortion. I chose the hospital route.

At the hospital I had to tell them I was married and that I had children to get the IUD. I wore a fake wedding ring. I made up a different menstrual history. I waited in a crowded waiting room for what seemed like an eternity. Finally my name was called, not my real name, of course.

The doctor examined me and asked several times, "Are you sure you're not pregnant?"

I tried to play it cool. "Of course not, there's no way I could be pregnant," I stammered, hoping he wouldn't see through my distress and frightened words. I was so scared—terrified that he wouldn't give me the IUD. To this day I don't know if he believed my lie about not being pregnant or if he sensed my desperation and was trying to help me.

Several hours after the insertion of the IUD I began to have uterine cramps, which became progressively more severe. It took five days for my body to complete the abortion process. Five days of agony. Five days of fighting off a fever and an infection. Finally it was over. My body began to heal. I felt numb—and relieved.

My abortion took place in an atmosphere of fear and desperation. I didn't know how to help myself feel strong and confident. I had little personal support and no societal support. Determined to end the pregnancy, I did what I needed to do.

I know how lucky I was to have survived that ordeal, how lucky I was not to have suffered a bad infection from that IUD, how lucky I was that I did not die. I know other women were not so lucky.

Through my personal experience of abortion and knowledge of my mother's experience, I have a visceral understanding of the experiences of other women. I can feel what they are going through. Not that their experience is exactly the same as mine, but it is similar enough to bond me to them.

I don't want what happened to my mother or me to happen to one other woman. I don't want either of my daughters or granddaughters to experience the fear and desperation I went through, nor do I want them to be subjected to physical and psychological indignities and dangers, or to be forced to bear children they don't want.

Women need the care and respect of the society in which they live. We need to be empowered and protected by society's laws—for childbirth and for the reality of undesired pregnancy. This reality includes the sometimes painful, often difficult process of deciding whether to continue a pregnancy.

Throughout history, women have borne the responsibility for bearing and raising children. This has included responsibility for deciding that not all pregnancies should be brought to term. It is unlikely that this will change any time soon, unless and until women's needs are recognized and met by society. The truth is we face many decisions about life alone.

Moral Responsibility

To bring life through the body or to turn it back is an awesome power of female human beings. It does not follow that because it is awesome it is to be feared. That women have internalized the patriarchy's fear of the power of physical processes, particularly pregnancy, is a sad commentary on female oppression.

The continuum of creative life includes death on all levels—intellectual as well as emotional, spiritual as well as physical. It is helpful, and perhaps essential, to adopt a positive attitude towards experiences that are transformational. Abortion is such an experience. Resistance to what is happening, or to what one is afraid will happen, deprives a person of the opportunity to be a willing partner in the transformation.

This is not by any means easy. Most people resist being in the center of their experience, fearing judgment and punishment. Often we don't trust our ability to discern and discriminate and make choices. We are unaccustomed to treating "bad" experiences as legitimate and important, as well as possibly meaningful to who we are and who we are becoming.

The nature of a woman's existence changes when she is pregnant. Shifts in her perception of herself and those around her can occur that affect her ability or desire to function in her daily life in the same ways she functioned before becoming pregnant. She may not see things the same way she did. She may become aware of new ways to see and understand what is going on in her life and what she believes about that.

The personal context of a crisis pregnancy occurs within the larger social context of a woman's life and society. It is unrealistic and a distortion to separate the morality of abortion from other moral and ethical issues.

Deciding to bring through or turn back a pregnancy is a female moral responsibility. We are charged with negotiating the ethics of relationship at the most primal level. A pregnant woman must face this *because* she is pregnant. To learn to exercise her responsibility a woman needs personal and societal support and respect for her authority to make procreative decisions. Scarcity of social support is the most significant contributor to psychological distress and confusion around abortion, especially in relation to morality and spirituality.

A pregnancy crisis confronts a woman with her personal psychology and all the constructs that influence the female personality in patriarchy. The belief that women shouldn't make decisions and shouldn't be in charge reinforces the difficulty we have making decisions.

Often our sense of ourselves as powerful beings is at odds with our self-image. We might try to reject it. As we learn to accept the legitimacy of our power we begin to attach a positive value to caring for ourselves as well as caring for those around us.

We learn that it is all right to make life decisions that favor our own growth. We grow to accept the idea that it is moral and ethical for us to benefit from having an abortion or a baby. We move from self-sacrifice to the conscious assertion of our personal power.

Conscious living means conscious choice making. Conscious choice making in pregnancy goes beyond biological realities. It encompasses the vastness of Life. An essential task for women is to learn to care about ourselves as individuals, and drop the bias we hold against ourselves, a bias we have internalized from a culture that is fundamentally antiwoman.

A society and culture that is antiwoman is antihuman. Male dominance in the reproductive life of our species distorts and limits the possibility for living life in peace, guided by love of life and people. It separates people instead of bringing them together. It denies men as well as women the truth of their identities as human beings. It is time to turn this around.

Life, Love, Motherhood, and Power

*At the Routh Street Women's Clinic we do sacred work
that honors women and the circle of life and death. When
you come here bring only love.*

—SIGN OUTSIDE A CLINIC IN TEXAS

WHEN EVA FIRST CAME TO TALK TO ME ABOUT AN ABORTION she had had the year before, she could barely say the word *abortion*. She felt ashamed that she had chosen to end the pregnancy. She referred to her abortion as "the time when I did that." She thought having an abortion was a sign of moral weakness and that she had "taken the easy way out." She believed she should have chosen to be a mother regardless of the harshness or difficulty she would have encountered had she become a single mother at the time of the pregnancy. Giving the baby up for adoption was unacceptable to her.

Interestingly, Eva reserved her harsh judgments for herself only, not for other women. She was young, in her twenties, and accustomed to operating in the world without support from others. She had reacted to the unexpected news of pregnancy by keeping mostly to herself and withholding what was going on from those close to her. Her decision to end her pregnancy came several weeks after she had initially decided to have the baby.

Eva's boyfriend did not want to remain in relationship with her, nor was he willing to help her with a baby. This was crushing news for her, for Eva placed the importance of relationships with men above all other relationships. She wanted to live her life in a traditional (patriarchal) family, and wouldn't allow herself to consider proceeding with the pregnancy without a man in the picture. She was completely convinced that any other way to live was a sign of moral failure. She held onto this ideal in her mind, even though the experiences of women around her revealed a variety of possible ways to build a family.

Many of us feel pressured to have an abortion when the alternative to it is single parenthood. We fear the now old-fashioned label of *unwed mother*. We can't tolerate the idea of our child being thought of as *illegitimate*. We don't want to risk becoming an outcast in relation to the rest of society. We find it impossible to overcome our sense that we will lose moral standing in the larger community, even if being alone with a child is an attractive alternative.

Eva was in a terrible bind. She felt obligated to continue her pregnancy in spite of her feelings about single motherhood. She planned for the birth of her child without thinking it through. She assumed that being pregnant necessarily meant giving birth and having a child. Her moral standards did not include choices once she was pregnant. It was okay with her for other women to have abortions, but it was not okay for her. Having an abortion meant that she was unmotherly, unfeminine, unwomanly. She felt weak and ashamed. She hated herself because she hadn't been willing to sacrifice her own welfare to her ideal of motherhood.

Eva believed she wasn't worthy enough to be a mother *and* that her unwillingness to sacrifice herself was a cruel act that had caused harm to another being. She had wanted to have the baby but decided to have an abortion because she didn't believe she deserved to have a baby. Through the process of having an abortion she punished herself for having become pregnant. She was not consciously aware that she was doing this. Her low self-esteem operated unconsciously to point her towards hurting herself. She believed that she should be punished for being unworthy and morally weak, and that her suffering was well deserved.

Unfortunately, Eva's attitude is not unusual. It's easy for women to get caught in a circle of ambiguity about self-worth. This can lead to romanticizing about how life could be different than it is, like thinking, *If I were a really good person I would have been willing to sacrifice myself to have a baby.*

A woman with a negative attitude towards herself might view an unintended or unwanted pregnancy as proof of her moral failure. Her inability to value her own feelings and needs will completely color her decision making process. If she decides to have an abortion, she is likely to see her reasons as invalid no matter what they are.

Unfortunately, because abortion is available without counseling about self-esteem, some women use their options in pregnancy to hurt themselves. If the choice of abortion is made out of self-hatred, she will suffer afterwards. If she is convinced of her unworthiness, she might never become aware of her real feelings about becoming a mother.

Counseling with Eva was troublesome and at times distressing. She refused to consider the idea that she could be as worthy of compassion and consideration as other women she knew who had made difficult pregnancy decisions. Any suggestion I made to that end was rejected. She clung to her harsh version of events and was unwilling to explore other possibilities. She embraced the sad bind she was in, and was unwilling to let it go, even though it caused her great emotional pain. My assertions that she could be gentler with herself and that her pain could be resolved were met with tearful resignation. She seemed afraid to find a way out of her misery. At the end, when we were unable to find a way out of her hopelessness, she ended our counseling relationship.

I do not fault Eva for the failure of counseling. She is not to blame, nor am I. Neither of us was able to reach deep enough into the well of feeling she presented. We didn't take enough risks or raise enough questions. I learned a lot about deep-seated social issues and how they take up residence in women's psyches, and lock horns with everything that matters. The way we want our lives to be becomes a dream deferred while we struggle to extract ourselves from our own tangled judgments.

Eva had an impact on my thinking about the struggle with abortion. The chasm between us, while impossible to cross, was instrumental in the growth of my appreciation for the tender pain that large historical and spiritual issues can ignite in the personal process of one woman. Knowing her for the short time that I did was humbling and made me a better counselor and a more compassionate thinker.

The choice to have an abortion flies in the face of the idea that it is good to sacrifice ourselves. It challenges us to accept our intrinsic power, and to make decisions about pregnancy and motherhood that are grounded in the reality of our everyday lives. However, it doesn't always work this way. Eva's story illustrates the tenacity of the ideology of self-sacrifice, and how it can influence a woman to remain a martyr to her own suffering.

Striving for peace of mind about abortion can feel like a life-and-death struggle. The psychological suffering of some women with abortion is testimony to the ferociousness of the struggle for freedom and equality. The old ways of thinking and being hold onto us as if they are all there is. We reach for greater awareness but it eludes our grasp.

Abortion, like birth, places women at life's doorway. Both are about the reproduction of life *and* the innate power of women. Our experience of pregnancy and abortion takes place in the context of historically evolving female identity. Within the personal experience of each woman lies an essential piece of the collective story of all women. Both women and men, personally and collectively, are moving away from a male-dominated, property-over-people society to a society that puts human needs and relationships first.

There are two main ways for human beings to live their lives: with self-awareness or without it. When we live without self-awareness, we often see ourselves as victims of circumstances. Living with self-awareness gives us the opportunity to take conscious responsibility for our lives. This can be difficult and demanding because, more often than not, we learn this kind of awareness through difficult and emotionally painful events. Living with self-awareness asks us to step back and be willing to observe ourselves.

When we step back from painful personal experiences and allow ourselves to see the bigger picture, we begin to see that our personal experiences are buffeted by the winds of larger social issues. We gain a historical perspective. We see that our personal situations are the direct result of centuries of human experience and that we can extricate ourselves from oppressive situations only to the degree that our society has changed to allow us to move to free ourselves. Then, as we free ourselves, society changes even more. It is a symbiotic personal/political dance in historical time.

We also gain psychological and spiritual perspectives. As we see the relationship between our personality patterns and behavior, and the timeless movement of our soul towards wholeness and connectedness, we gain a sense that life is meaningful. Once we open to the realm of soul and spirit, it is no longer possible to experience life only on the physical or mental level.

Abortion has the power to wound. It also offers opportunities for immeasurable personal growth and healing. The emotional pain of the experience allows women to open to themselves in ways not otherwise possible. It often pushes a woman to a deeply introspective place where a great deal of personal learning can occur. Having an abortion, though painful, can act as a catalyst for a woman to become more aware of her personal power. When we come face to face with our life-giving power we also encounter our authority and capacity as women. We're offered a different image of ourselves than the one given to us by patriarchy. Intrinsic strength steps forward to replace societally imposed weakness.

The capacity to bring life through the body is a significant part of female existence. The guidance and control of this capacity is part of women's consciousness. Even if pregnancy is never experienced physically, the capacity for it puts women in a uniquely feminine relationship to the world. The process of giving life is powerful and transformative, and innately creative. As it occurs within the female body and psyche, it is a matter of female power and responsibility.

The nature of intrinsic power, life-determining power, the power of being, is different from the way we usually think of power. It is "the power we sense in a seed, in the growth of a child, the power we feel writing, weaving, working, creating, making choices..."[1] Intrinsic power is the manifestation of our genuine nature. It is the expression of our truth. It has nothing to do with subjugation of the environment or other people.

We actively express female power when we choose whether to bring pregnancy through or turn it back. As women have the power to give life, so do we have the power to withhold the giving. When pregnancy is turned back, its creative essence can be expressed in other ways. Pregnancy promises the continuity of life and the coming of new life. Abortion redirects the process, turns it back on itself, and returns it to the Earth.

The history of patriarchy includes an ongoing effort to control this aspect of women's lives. Women have responded, personally and historically, by trying to regain social control over the power to create life. When we consciously assert our power to regulate biological reproduction we see ourselves exercising our life-creating power. When we see ourselves in terms of our personal power we are likely to become convinced that *we* must be the primary moral authority in matters that concern our bodies and our relationship to the life-creating process of pregnancy.

Legal, freely chosen abortion recognizes women's control over which humans will emerge into the physical world and which will not. It places the power of feminine energy firmly inside the human female instead of in some realm external to her. However, an individual human female, carrying the effects of thousands of years of male-dominated society, is likely to feel psychologically unprepared to manage this power. When she comes face to face with it, she might feel overwhelmed and frightened.

An unexpected pregnancy, especially if it is unwanted, brings anxiety with it. Personal issues about nurturing and abandonment rise to the surface. A centuries old obligation to carry through any pregnancy can color and complicate both a woman's desire to be a mother *and* her emotional connection to a possible child. Women feel these obligations as psychological pressure. The leading emotion is guilt. The source of the pressure is historical and societal, but most women take it on as their own isolated personal problem.

The Unity of Birth and Death

When a woman has an abortion she senses that someone or something has died. There is no turning away from the presence of profound change, even if it is a potentiality rather than an actuality that has passed. Given the nature of abortion, it is natural that increased awareness about the place of death in life grows out of the experience.

Few people in our culture are comfortable with thinking or talking about death. We have lost our sense of connection to it. We mystify it and deny it at the same time, and have great difficulty taking responsibility for it. But, facing both physical and psychological death allows us to be real with ourselves.

Change is a form of death. We often fear it as well. We forget that change is a constant in Life and that it is to be expected. We can learn to dance with change instead of resisting or fighting it. Most of us live lives that are shielded from the natural world. Our dependence on technology fools us into thinking we can control the flow of death and change in our lives. Our highly technological, alienated-from-nature culture fears death and anxiously guards an abstract idea of life.

Nature shows us that a central aspect of Life is its ever-changingness. Life moves into death, moves into life, and into death again. This is most easily observed in the cycle of the seasons: fall to winter to spring to summer to fall to winter again. The leaves on the trees die and are reborn and die and are reborn and die and are reborn. Nature does not judge nor care about the outcome. For Nature, death is an acceptable, necessary, and sometimes desirable part of Life.

When a woman chooses to abort a pregnancy she engages in this primal dance, the turning of the Wheel of Life. And, because it is a natural turning, no amount of effort on the part of the patriarchal powers that be has been able to obliterate it.

Women today, more than ever before, are acting in their own interests. We are searching to understand and take responsibility for the dimension of our lives that calls for us to end life in order to preserve and support Life. As we experience choice in pregnancy we come closer to understanding our relationships in Life. Through acknowledging the unity of birth and death in abortion we come to more fully understand the nature of Creation.

It is important to face the issue of death in abortion. There is no need to hide from the fact that death is part of the experience. Unfortunately, the political framework of abortion puts many of us who support legal abortion on the defensive with regard to the death involved.

Much of the pain of abortion comes from the denial of death or the misinterpretation of the nature of that death. One of the reasons some of us have difficulty with abortion, and why the experience does not feel resolved, is because we deny that any death has occurred. If we do acknowledge a death, we might consider the death to be bad and believe that we are guilty of killing or murder.

That it could be possible for death in abortion to occur without killing, or that killing in life might be natural under certain circumstances, is almost impossible to understand in our current ways of thinking. But we need to question these black and white, either/or, moralistic ways of thinking to adequately honor the truth of abortion.

In Webster's *Collegiate Dictionary*, the word *kill* "merely states the fact of death caused by an agency in any manner *(killed in an accident)* *(frost killed the plants)*." So goes the dispassionate dictionary definition. The words *ending life* are undoubtedly easier for most of us than the word *killing*, but softening concepts is not helpful when it comes to being honest about what we are really dealing with.

If we dare to grapple with the word *killing* in relation to abortion, we have to distance ourselves from any strong emotions that might subvert our objectivity. But, is it possible to be objective about pregnancy, mothering, and babies—subjects that provoke our most heartfelt emotions? I'm suggesting that we *must* be objective if we want to get to the bottom of our struggle with ourselves. The more clear-eyed we can be, the more we have a chance to resolve our difficulties.

In doing research for this book I came across another book, *Mother Nature: A History of Mothers, Infants, and Natural Selection*, by anthropologist Sarah Blaffer Hrdy. In it, she makes a strong case for a broad range of evolutionary possibilities with regard to the reproductive behavior of women. She suggests that the various ways women have consistently acted to control and direct reproductive events are basic to the evolution of the human race. Included in this, along with normal nurturing and abortion, are abandonment and infanticide, which in today's world are considered extreme decisions but in centuries past have not been seen that way.

"These consistencies remind us that we descend from creatures for whom the timing of reproduction has always made an enormous difference, and that the physiological and motivational underpinnings of a quintessentially 'pro-choice' mammal are not new." [2]

A quintessentially "pro-choice" mammal. The phrase rings in my mind. Sarah Hrdy emphasizes the crucial role of context in the history of the reproductive decision making of our species. She also includes other animals and insects in the scope of her wide scientific lens. In Nature, she teaches us, we can find examples of the reabsorption of embryos into the body of female animals, and the culling of litters to allow the strongest infant animals to survive (infanticide, to be sure).

Included in this list are beetles, spiders, fish, birds, mice, ground squirrels, prairie dogs, wolves, bears, lions, tigers, hippopotami, and wild dogs. The organic wisdom of female members of many species shows a common pattern of selective killing under specific circumstances in order to serve Life. Hrdy goes on to say that even infanticide is adaptive in some circumstances, and she includes primates, which includes humans, in this generalization.[3] Then, she reminds us that "abortion—especially in the early stages of pregnancy—is safer for the mother than giving birth. No one with other options chooses infanticide."[4]

The California mouse, a socially monogamous rodent, will eliminate its offspring if there is no help from a male to rear them. In other types of rodents the female will end pregnancy prior to birth if she senses a potentially dangerous male in her vicinity. She will reabsorb her embryos, what Hrdy calls "this efficient form of early-stage abortion."[5] Pregnant monkeys, like humans, are unable to reabsorb their embryos, but they can spontaneously abort if there is a threat to their situation or social group.[6]

So, what does the reproductive life of nonhuman animals have to do with us? Specifically, what does all this have to do with the morality of abortion? I think that opening our minds to knowing about the history of our species, especially in relation to other species, can help us understand where our experiences with abortion fit in the larger scheme of things.

The reality of All Life is concretely illustrated in scientific studies of Earth's creatures. Concepts that might appear to be only spiritual or nonmaterial turn out, on closer examination, to have scientific significance. The Interrelationship of All Life, the spiritual perspective held by indigenous peoples and the original people—the ancestors of *all* people—is a foundational ecological truth, though we encounter it mainly in spiritual contexts. Each life form is dependent on other life forms for its existence. Each cannot thrive without the other. Decisions to turn life back, to cause death, to reabsorb, to *kill* if you will, whether organically or mindfully made, make sense only in the context of the relationships that define the circumstances of particular times, places, and persons.

If we add human consciousness to an unstable pregnancy equation we come up with an entirely different scenario, a uniquely human one. Granted, we can't *physically* reabsorb a fetus, but we can reabsorb it *energetically*. If a woman perceives that her pregnancy is unstable, that it is unsupported by the rest of her life, she can act to have it removed from her body. But what happens emotionally, mentally, and spiritually? Human beings are fourfold creatures. We don't just do things physically. We seek to integrate our body, mind, soul, and spirit, in our daily lives and in pursuit of our dreams. What do we do with the emotional, mental, and spiritual energy of an aborted pregnancy?

We reabsorb it. We transform it. We take it back into ourselves and make it into something else. We do it in a way that is unique to being a human female, a woman. It is part of our nature to do this. There is nothing unnatural about it.

The issue of killing in abortion must be addressed from the point of view of our fourfold nature and in terms of the fullness of woman's creative nature. We don't *kill* in a coldhearted, malicious, or thoughtless way when we have an abortion. Nor are we disconnected from what we are doing. We take life back into itself, because that is our role and our destiny. That is the body-mind-soul-spirit we were given by Earth. We must learn to own this intimate power, know our true nature, and take our place in the pantheon of being.

In an abortion, the developing fetus is separated from its source of growth, the pregnant woman. This occurs as a result of the woman's conscious decision not to nurture the fetus. The idea that the death of the fetus is bad or that injury or injustice has somehow been perpetrated against the fetus causes much suffering and confusion. For some women, like Eva, it is agonizing.

Life cries out to us to reexamine our attitude towards death and make room for a new, more positive way of thinking. Our personal and societal fear of the end of life makes us label any kind of death *bad.* A walk in Nature will quickly correct this notion. Let's look again at the dynamic ecosystem that is a forest. Disturbances that occur within the forest, such as fire, insects, diseases, and weather storms are considered *agents of change.* An agent of change in Nature brings about the death or metamorphosis of one organism so that others can come into being and allow the whole system to survive. A naturally caused fire in a wilderness area might be desirable under certain circumstances because it brings balance to the system as a whole.

When we allow ourselves to entertain the idea that there is nothing necessarily bad about death, we can begin to open to the multifaceted truth of
our experience and release ourselves from the bind of self-condemning
thinking. It is vital that we have clarity about our deeper intentions when
we choose to have an abortion. We can bring loving attention to bear on
our pregnancy choices if we are clear that our personal circumstances fit
into the choice to end life in order to preserve and support Life. The key is
to bring our own lives into a place of equal status with all other life. Not
superior, just equal.

The right to life of a woman is not a right *over* the right of the fetus to
life. We are charged in pregnancy with the responsibility of *balancing* life
in the context of the reality of our relationships as they have been presented
to us so far. The choice to allow death to occur through abortion is an expression of women's creative life-giving power in action.

Compassion

This prayer by an anonymous woman was printed in *Conscience,* the
newsletter of the remarkable group, Catholics For Choice:

> I AM GOING TO HAVE AN ABORTION, —GOD—and I feel
> terribly alone. FOR SO OFTEN MY FAITH HAS CON-
> DEMNED MY DECISION; and members of my faith have
> threatened me with expulsion; and others have reviled, cursed,
> called me "murderer"—for this that I must do.
>
> I have read the theological arguments and the philosophical
> debates against abortion, so frequently and so loudly proclaimed
> as God's Trust. But from them I hear only of the concern for the
> yet unborn life—I find no concern for the lives of those who face
> the valley of despair.
>
> And the loneliness I and my family feel as we live through
> these long and difficult days of waiting is eased only by the
> knowledge that You are here close beside us and that You are

concerned for us. As in Your Word we find hope, and joy, and peace; and an honesty to face the responsibilities and decisions we must make.

It is lonely not to be able to share this awful time with even closest friends and loved ones—but we cannot risk the hatred. And I cannot risk rejection. So I face them with a false smile upon my life, and a false cheerfulness answers their most asked question, "How are you?"

God, forgive my bitterness and anger at their coldness and prejudice. Help me to find a way to breach this deep valley that now separates us. Help me pray in your words, "forgive them, for they know not what they do."

For they cannot walk in my shoes, or know the point of my breaking. It was an act of love that began this unwanted growth, and a decision of love that will end it. For I am too old to bear another child. I already have five at home for whom I am responsible. One of these is severely handicapped and retarded, and I can not forsake her future needs of me. And the other four still need much from me in love, and care, and attention, and time.

God, I cannot handle more.[7]

Compassion, that singular facet of human nature, has been sorely lacking in the fundamentalist religious war on abortion rights. Doctrinaire views and ignorant fears often combine in the minds of people who would like the world to be a lot simpler than it is. I remember a woman with whom I once shared a panel debating about abortion. She spoke passionately against it. "Death is death," she declared with the tinge of a shriek lining her unilateral pronouncement.

There is no context for death? I wondered. It just happens in the abstract and is always the same no matter what? War death? Disease death? Accidental death? Death from suicide? Death from murder? Death from assassination? Death from execution? Natural death? They're all the same? I don't think so.

Death happens in specific circumstances, and there is always a story to go with it. There is always a context for it. And it carries different meanings depending on the nature of its relationship to the people who give it meaning.

What struck me most about my panel partner was her absolute lack of compassion for the women whose most intimate needs would be affected by whether abortion was legal and safe. She seemed to think of herself as completely separate and different from them and thus had no difficulty finding fault with their choices. The more I took in what she was saying, the more I realized that I needed to dig more deeply to understand where her fear was coming from and how I might be able to broaden my own perspective to clear up some of the perplexities and misunderstandings around abortion.

We mustn't let ourselves think in narrow, simplistic terms just to justify our own position in life. We must imagine what it's like to be another person, why that person lives as she does, and how we can expand our own thinking to take in aspects of her experience that are unfamiliar and scary to us. Compassion asks us to be willing to step into another person's shoes and really grasp what is happening to her and why she might make the kinds of choices she's making. If it's not possible to walk in her shoes, compassion asks us to withhold judgment anyway.

Life and Pregnancy

Only a woman's body is able to produce and sustain the process of growth and development essential to the reproduction of human beings on Earth—pregnancy. It would seem to logically follow that only she would be in charge of the process. However, because of the nature of sexual relations between women and men at this point in human development and the way power in society is organized, this logical assumption has become skewed. As a result, we often feel we have little or no control over the occurrence of pregnancy.

Once a pregnancy takes hold physically, it takes on terms and characteristics familiar to most of us. *Zygote, embryo, fetus, fertilization,* and *im-*

plantation are some of these. The process engages a woman's body completely. The nausea and fatigue that many women experience during the first part of pregnancy serve as bold reminders of this fact.

Trying to pin down a process is not easy, because it is always moving. We mark the passages in the process of pregnancy by attributing significance to ideas like conception and birth in order to fit the process into the social system in which we live. While not scientifically based, they often carry much personal meaning. But, life never begins or ends. It continues, manifesting in an ever-changing array of forms.

"So far as genes and tissue are concerned, embryo-fetus-baby represents a biological continuum. No distinction can be other than arbitrary. In this sense, the transition between fetus and personhood is no less ambiguous today than it was a hundred thousand years ago." [8]

Again, the female body is the context in which the development of life in pregnancy occurs. Our bodies exist within the context of our lives and our awareness of our lives. The changes that take place biologically are reflected in our awareness of them. Advancing medical technologies, such as ultrasound and other monitoring devices, that augment our ability to perceive the inner workings of the body, are altering our awareness. We're looking at our insides from the outside, as if we were away from ourselves. We rely less on our own senses and more on what we are shown by medical technology. Still, when it comes down to it, we must rely on ourselves to know how we truly feel about being pregnant. The facts of biological life often take a back seat when we are pressed to decide whether to continue a pregnancy.

Development and relatedness are the ongoing terms with which to understand pregnancy—biologically, psychologically, socially, and spiritually. A fetus becomes distinctly human at about the same time it can survive outside the womb. Biological research tells us that this is around twenty-four to thirty-two weeks of pregnancy. However, the march of medical science has made this a murky area.

And so I say again, the developmental stages of pregnancy need women to define their status in life. Their biological status relative to other species of life is not distinctly human until late in pregnancy and after birth.[9] They have no "rights." (We don't either.) They have only their organic and spiritual connection to All Life. The whole concept of rights in relation to Life is a false idea. Nature doesn't work that way, and we are part of Nature. Nature operates in context, in relationship. If we have any rights at all they are rights to be in natural relationship with each other and with the land, air, water, and creatures of Earth. We should put our effort into supporting a morality of right relationship that supports individuals, rather than individual rights divorced from relationships.

How a woman relates to a pregnancy and the different stages of pregnancy will depend upon all the interacting elements of her personality and her life situation. Her experience of death in abortion will most likely stimulate her to feel the depth of her connection to loving relationships in her life. The process is often stunning in its power to reveal how complicated and ambiguous these can be. Women with whom I have spoken have told me that their hearts opened when they had abortions. They felt inspired by their experience to recognize the most important people in their lives in new ways, sometimes for the first time.

We don't usually make our decision whether to have an abortion on the basis of anyone's abstract right to life. We make our decision on the basis of whether care for the child will be adequate. Inevitably this includes the level of caring we feel for the fetus, baby, or child. (Words we choose to use reflect our feelings.) We look at whether we are emotionally prepared to care. We look at the effect of the pregnancy on our life and the effect of life's circumstances on the child.

Nitty Gritty Love

Life in pregnancy is meaningful only as it exists in relation to life already born. It has no abstract meaning. A life form is not meaningful because it is life. It is meaningful only in relation to other life forms that nurture its existence.

That means that love must be in the picture somewhere. Not abstract love, or generalized love, or religious love. The love that needs to be present to bring forth life from women's bodies is a kind of love I call *nitty gritty love.*

Nitty gritty love supports us to get up in the middle of the night to tend to the needs of a new life. It is the kind of love that gives a person the willingness to sacrifice personal needs and desires to the unpredictability of a baby's calling. It is the kind of love we feel only sometimes in our lives. It cannot be artificially induced or forced. It cannot be socially pressured. It is either there or not. If it is not there or only partially there, a woman has every reason to consider discontinuing a pregnancy.

For most women choosing to have an abortion is a loving, caring act.

A woman might exercise her love and care to end a pregnancy because of external or internal circumstances, or a combination of the two, which she decides are unsafe or unsupportive of a new life. It is our sense of responsibility for life that usually plays a central role in decision making about pregnancy.

Pregnancy, when it is unwanted, can be life threatening. It might threaten a woman's spiritual, psychological, and physical well-being, which in turn, if she is already a mother, could threaten the well-being of her born children. If she continues an unwanted pregnancy, her ability to care for all her children might be compromised because she has spread herself too thin.

The Institution of Motherhood

Rape and its aftermath; marriage as economic dependence, as the guarantee to a man of "his" children; the theft of childbirth from women; the concept of the "illegitimacy" of a child born out of wedlock; the laws regulating contraception and abortion; the cavalier marketing of dangerous birth control devices; the denial that work done by women at home is a part of "production"; the chaining of women in links of love and guilt; the absence of social benefits for mothers; the inadequacy of childcare facilities in most parts of the world; the un-equal pay women receive as wage-earners, forcing them often into de-pendence on a man; the solitary confinement of "full-time motherhood"; the token nature of fatherhood, which gives a man rights and privileges over children toward whom he assumes minimal respon-sibility; the psychoanalytic castigation of the mother; the pediatric as-sumption that the mother is inadequate and ignorant; the burden of emotional work borne by women in the family—all these are connect-ing fibers of this invisible institution, and they determine our relation-ship to our children whether we like to think so or not. [10]

Only a little has changed since Adrienne Rich wrote those words. That women are able to experience the joys of motherhood within the institu-tion of motherhood is a tribute to our ability to push beyond narrow defi-nitions. It is a reflection of our ability to maintain a sense of community within oppressive social structures, as well as to preserve a love-centered mother-child relationship.

Interestingly, it is often in outcast minority subcultures that the insti-tution of motherhood least affects the personal status of a pregnant woman. In many poor communities, children are embraced regardless of their "legitimacy."

The flip side of that is a tragic paradox of reasoning in the mind of a (usu-ally young) woman who feels discarded by society. She adopts a "bad" identity and tries to be as "bad" as possible, because she derives her self-esteem from being "bad," and because that is her perception of what is ex-pected of her by the dominant culture. Someone who is caught up in this way of thinking might relish the idea of having a child outside of society's rules.

At the height of Victorian prudery in the last two centuries, if a woman did not marry she was at risk to "fall" into prostitution, especially if she was of the working class. Remaining single was not an economic option for most women. An unmarried woman was not looked upon as *single* until the last

part of the twentieth century. She was seen as *unwed*. If she remained unmarried, she could count on being labeled an *old maid* or a *spinster*.

Attitudes about single women and pregnancy have changed for the better in the last thirty years or so, thanks to the women's movement. *Single
mother* or *single parent* has, for the most part, replaced *unwed mother*. Not
at all coincidentally, the shift in attitudes and language began after 1973,
when abortion was legalized throughout the country.

"Many women in the United States who got legal abortions or became
single mothers in the 1970s felt that their newly won ability to control their
fertility gave them a degree of independence and dignity." [11]

Today it's easier for women to choose to be single. There is less risk of
being socially ostracized for having sex outside of marriage. But social and
economic realities change in bumpy and uneven ways, and large numbers
of women in the United States continue to feel pressured to marry for economic security and social status. In some parts of the world, women are
killed for what are considered violations of "family honor."

In patriarchal social relations, women and children get their legitimacy
from their recognized attachment to a man. Simply stated, this is the belief
that a woman should be married when she conceives and bears a child, and
that the child belongs to her husband. This is the root of the misogynist
male fear of being "trapped." An unmarried pregnant woman who desires
or feels forced by circumstances to be a mother might try to manipulate a
man to support her since to go it alone is often a road to poverty and hardship. Inequality, fear, and unbalanced dependency often combine to produce dishonesty in sexual relationships.

The idea of an *unwed mother* and an *illegitimate child* comes from the denial of the primacy of the mother-child relationship. It is an idea that serves
to enforce and reinforce a male-centered focus for the family. It recognizes
the role of the father as supreme.

Only a generation ago, a child whose mother was not legally tied to its
father was given a lowered social status. A woman who mothered a child
on her own, without a binding attachment to a man was considered to be

less socially respectable. Her sexuality was considered legitimate only if it occurred within marriage, where she was wedded to and identified by a man. A child born to a woman who was labeled an unwed mother was tainted by its mother's shame. This shaming of women was a powerful means of controlling behavior with regard to choices made about pregnancy.

Single mothers on welfare are some of the most vulnerable and least protected people in our society today. A woman who is economically dependent on the state for her children's life and health is often the first to have her choices in pregnancy limited by restricted funding and regulations that deny her good pre-natal and maternity care, and access to abortion. She is often encouraged or coerced to use high-risk methods of birth control or to be sterilized. If she is poor *and* a woman of color this will be even truer.

Her ability to make choices and control her reproductive life is not respected. She is punished for being without a man and for being poor. The treatment she receives from public agencies set up to support her is often disrespectful and demeaning. Victimized by society, she is punished for being a victim.

According to the rules of patriarchy and the institution of motherhood, any expression of female sexuality that occurs independent of male authority is considered unnatural and deviant. Thus, women who engage in premarital sex (the term itself assumes we will all marry) have been labeled *bad, dirty, promiscuous, whores,* or *sluts.* While society has become more open about female sexuality, prejudiced attitudes and assumptions remain.

The categories established by the institution of motherhood place men instead of women in the center of the pregnancy experience because they measure the status of pregnancy according to the location of a man in a woman's life. This distorts our perception of our own experience. To know that not only could we be socially ostracized, but our child might be punished as well, is a strong incentive not to go against the dominant morality.

Thus, we may choose to have an abortion because we (unconsciously or consciously) fear the power of the institution of motherhood to label us as unwed or bad and our children as illegitimate. We might also fear the loss of support, both emotional and financial, that we could incur as a result of continuing a pregnancy as a single person.

While we might feel socially pressured to have an abortion, we might also feel that we don't want to be a mother at the time of a particular pregnancy. We will be shamed for this as well since the institution of motherhood demands that all women want to be mothers. It is motherhood that gives women personhood in patriarchal culture and society. It is considered deviant for a woman not to want to be a mother.

Lesbians have been considered deviant for wanting, or not wanting, to be mothers. Those of us who define ourselves and our relationships with children in our own terms receive little support for our choices.

Some women choose to continue pregnancies to avoid the social stigma and negative self-esteem we associate with having an abortion. We choose to give birth because that is what we believe we are supposed to do, even though it might not be what we truly wish to do.

Many women look forward to being mothers. We accept the responsibilities eagerly and do everything we can to care for our children.

Some women fear the possible constriction and contraction of our lives and personalities if we were to try to fit ourselves into the limited definitions of womanhood imposed on us by the institution of motherhood. Unable to see our way clear to experience motherhood freely, we choose not to experience it at all.

Some women do not desire to be mothers at any time. It is just as normal and natural not to want to be a mother as it is to want to be a mother.

Abortion is an intrinsic part of the collective experience of women with motherhood. As abortion negates the prospect of motherhood, so does it affirm its power. Abortion freely chosen brings into question the idea that it is motherhood that gives women their identity. It raises the possibility for women to determine their own personal experience of motherhood, rather than having our destiny determined for us by the institution of motherhood.

It can be emotionally painful to examine these issues. When we see that we have let others define our experience for us, we also see that we have denied the importance of our own lives and our full humanity. Rising to the surface as well might be a longing to be loved unconditionally and a sense of how that is missing in our lives.

The Ideal of the All-Loving Mother

The abstract assertion that a woman "should always want her baby," is an expression of an ideal: the ideal of the all-loving mother, the woman who is accepting of any and all pregnancies and who lives only to care for her children. No matter when, or how many, or under what circumstances her pregnancies occurred, the ideal mother would always "want her baby." She would care very little for herself, always putting the interests of her children first. She would give of herself "unselfishly" and never complain of hardship or unmet personal needs.

Ideally, she would have no personal needs other than to be a good mother. No sacrifice would be too great, especially if not sacrificing meant that her children would suffer. This saint-like, self-sacrificing mother is elevated to a divine status, but in earthly reality she is denied her human status and her human needs.

The all-loving mother ideal is a defensive patriarchal reaction to the regenerative power of the Earth. All beings and things partake of this earthly energy and all of us depend upon it. But, it does not flow freely through our lives and relationships, because human society is organized to try to contain and dominate this force. Mother Love is an all-consuming, endless stream of universal energy that supports life in its many forms and expressions. It is channeled through the human body and psyche as well as through the whole Earth. Confined within the boundaries of ideal yearnings and patriarchal forms it is continuously aborted as it seeks expression.

The assertion that every woman should want every pregnancy is an expression of the fears many people carry about being unwanted or unloved. It blames mothers, and all women, for not providing the unconditional love that we all crave.

Unfortunately, but understandably, women internalize this idea. We blame ourselves for not giving enough. We buy into the ideology of motherhood that both elevates female function beyond the human and strips female people of their humanity. The conflicts we encounter around abortion reflect the social and historical contradictions of the times in which we live. That is why the experience of abortion is profound.

We live in a time when a compelling urge is sweeping through large numbers of women to join womanhood and motherhood with full personhood. Implicit in legal abortion is the idea that there is more to being a woman than having children. Freely chosen abortion exposes the difference between motherhood freely chosen and the institution of motherhood, which imposes social roles and rules of relationship and does not allow the expression of individual will. It teaches us that, while having children can be a significant and natural expression of womanhood, not having children might be just as significant and natural.

If we choose to resolve a pregnancy through abortion, we are expressing our power to return our body to its natural nonpregnant state. If we choose to resolve a pregnancy through birth, we are expressing our personal power to remain in the natural pregnant state.

Women make choices within the context of a society that is hostile to our choice making. Pressures come from within and without. We make our choices within the limits of our awareness. We do the best we can.

Empowerment and Pain

As wise women and men in every culture tell us:
The art of life is not controlling what happens to us,
but using what happens to us.

—GLORIA STEINEM, *REVOLUTION FROM WITHIN*

I REMEMBER THE FIRST TIME PAULA CALLED ON THE PHONE. She said she was pregnant and that she didn't want to have a baby or an abortion. There was a wildness in her voice and a subtle sense of desperation hanging around the edges of her sentences. She seemed to be trying to maintain a calm tone to avoid being overwhelmed by panic.

The next day, sitting in the counseling room her eyes betrayed a certain apprehension about being there. "I can't believe this is happening to me," she said, revealing her fragility and sense of unreality.

I asked her how it would be to have a baby now. Her eyes filled with tears. She looked away. We sat together in silence while she began to release some of her pain and confusion.

"I'd really like to have a baby, but this isn't a good time. Is there ever a good time? I mean I'm almost thirty. I had an abortion three years ago and

I didn't have any problems. I just went in and had it done. But this time is different. I don't know why I'm so upset."

Paula and Rob, her boyfriend of two years, had not been getting along. She said things had been good between them up until the last six months or so. She didn't feel that she could rely on him to stay with her and help with the care of a baby.

"It's so easy for him," she said angrily. "What does he know, he's a guy."

I asked if she had told him she wanted to have a baby. She hadn't. She told him she was pregnant, no more than that. He told her he didn't want to have a baby, but that it was up to her. That was the extent of their interaction.

Paula felt it wouldn't do any good to talk to Rob, that he wouldn't understand and wouldn't be supportive of her. I thought to myself how sad this was, sad that two people could be in intimate relationship and have relatively little desire or ability to communicate. I knew it was not unusual.

"It scares me to think about having the baby on my own and being a single parent," Paula said quickly in response to my next question. I told Paula about support services in town, about Social Services, about a low cost community prenatal clinic, and about a support group a friend of mine was running for pregnant women.

Paula made it clear that none of these suggestions interested her. The more I talked about ways for her to have a baby the more she resisted the idea. It was becoming clear to both of us that a significant part of her was not at all interested in having a baby and that she was in the process of arguing for an abortion.

But another strong part of her did not want an abortion, especially another abortion. While she had no problems a few years before, she felt bad about herself for having "gotten myself into this again." The part of her that thought she should have a baby and that she should not have another abortion had set up a mental roadblock in her decision making process.

A chorus of internal *shoulds* confused and pressured her. Part of her said she should have a baby because she was pregnant and that every woman should want to have a baby. Part of her said that if she really loved her boyfriend she should want to have his baby. Part of her was saying that since she allowed herself to become pregnant she should pay for her mistake by having the baby. Part of her truly wanted to have a baby.

Paula was more emotionally connected with this pregnancy than she had been with the one before. She was a few years older and more in touch with her desire to have children. What was holding her back this time was the sense that this wasn't a good time.

"I don't want to bring a baby into the world under these circumstances," she insisted. "It just isn't right."

It just isn't right, is a moral statement about feeling responsible for another life. The morality of abortion for most women operates within the context of relationship. This might be a relationship with a man, a woman, family, children, work, the world, her body, herself, the pregnancy, or to the fetus, baby, or child, depending on our point of view.

Pregnancy is a natural condition of emotional, spiritual, mental, and physical relationship. The quality of relationship in pregnancy differs from one pregnancy to another and one woman to another.

While a woman is never completely separate from the fetus she is carrying, she will experience its existence differently according to her personal belief system, her emotional maturity and stability, her life experience, and the circumstances in which she finds herself at the time of a particular pregnancy. Her experience often encompasses aspects of both the pro-choice and pro-life political positions.

It is natural and normal to have mixed feelings about any pregnancy.

It is just as natural for a woman not to want to be pregnant as to want to be pregnant. It is natural and normal that women carry a full range of attitudes and feelings about pregnancy. The range spans all the way from the joy of a long awaited planned pregnancy to the degrading horror of a pregnancy from rape.

One woman might perceive her pregnancy as a mass of cells while another imagines it as a full-fledged baby. One woman might separate from her pregnancy easily, with a minimum of emotion, and another find herself so torn up that she can barely function. Another woman might become aware of her feelings about an abortion many years after it took place.

For a good number of women, the choice to have an abortion is straightforward. It does not provoke a personal crisis, nor does it interfere significantly with daily functioning. For others it is more problematic. External and internal pressures and obstacles combine to create confusion and a sense of being personally threatened. Thus, having an abortion can be emotionally painful, but like other difficult experiences it holds many possibilities for personal growth and healing.

Healing the pain of abortion means discovering the significance of pregnancy and abortion in a woman's life and doing the work of emotional and mental reorganization to integrate the experience positively in her identity and her life. Since, in the United States and some other countries, abortion has been legally recognized by society, it is now possible for women to embrace it as a legitimate part of their growth and development.

Personal struggles with abortion occur within women's ongoing efforts to know and understand themselves better. These struggles are part of the evolution of female power in society. We can no more avoid them than we can stop the flow of history. Some of the main psychological issues are:

- Feeling selfish and bad when we focus on ourselves
- Discounting and disparaging the self, otherwise known as low self-esteem
- Finding it difficult to initiate action
- Feeling conflicted about relationships and the value of caring
- Feeling unsure of our moral power

Why We Feel Bad About Ourselves

Beliefs about personal inferiority are rooted in social and economic systems of dominance and subordination. Our society values certain people over others. Individual qualities and characteristics do not determine the divisions. Here are a few of the prejudicial, divisive attitudes woven through the basic fabric of our society:

- Those who own and control economic production are considered more important than those who do not (capitalism).
- White people of Anglo-European descent are considered more important than those of other ethnic backgrounds (white supremacist racism).
- Men are considered more important than women (patriarchal sexism).

Subordinate groups have adopted and internalized these ideas. For example, many women accept the belief that we are not as important as men. Often we are not aware that we believe this. We develop assumptions, and don't question our beliefs or behavior. In practical terms this can mean that women find it difficult to act in their own interests and sometimes don't even know what those interests are.

Because women's experiences are often invalidated, we discount what we know to be true. We think we are making too much of something, or not enough, or that we don't know what we are talking about. No matter how competent or intelligent a woman might be, it is likely she will be plagued by a vague (or not-so-vague) sense of not belonging, of being illegitimate, or unentitled. When our experiences are devalued, it is natural for women to feel bad about themselves.

Throughout our lives we receive conflicting messages about sex and sexuality. Almost all of us have experienced ourselves as sexual objects and many of us have been sexually abused.

Because identity as a woman becomes more pronounced with pregnancy, unresolved issues about sex often come to the surface of a woman's awareness, particularly during a crisis pregnancy. Confusion and mixed feelings about being a sexual person stir up confusion about being a woman. As pregnancy makes a woman's sexual identity more evident she might feel bad about herself for being sexual.

Although it is legal in the United States, abortion is not generally acknowledged as a legitimate experience. Consequently many women feel they must hide their experience with abortion. Shame about having an abortion can precipitate an identity crisis about being a woman. The implications of this could resonate into all her relationships and life choices.

Choosing for Self

Carol Gilligan writes: "When uncertainty about her own worth prevents a woman from claiming equality, self-assertion falls prey to the old criticism of selfishness." [12]

Women fear being selfish. Given the choice between ourselves, our own needs, or others and their needs, most women attend to the needs of others.

Women's decisions about abortion take place in the context of male-centered morality, which devalues women's personal worth while, at the same time, it idealizes our role as nurturers and caretakers.

When women internalize this antifeminine morality—and inevitably we do—we distrust the value and validity of our own experiences and self-worth. We question not only our beliefs and ideas, but also our right to have them. We adopt the idea that we aren't caring for others if we care for ourselves.

The choice of abortion challenges woman's role in society and the ideology of self-sacrifice on which that role is based. It suggests that it is possible to make choices that enhance self-worth *and* are caring towards others. For many women, choosing an abortion is an exercise in challenging the ideology that tells us that caring for ourselves is bad.

For a woman to choose her own life first goes against everything we have been taught in patriarchy. Our moral conflicts about abortion are as much about the value of our own lives as they are about the value of the life of a fetus.

A woman who wishes to have an abortion often carries a deeply held, frequently unconscious belief, that to choose in favor of her own self-interest is morally wrong. She might be unable to resolve this, and in choosing abortion, choose to live with her guilt. *The guilt is not primarily about denying the life of a child, but rather that she did not deny herself.*

To the extent that a woman values her own needs she will be able to validate her right to act in her own self-interest. The more negatively she sees
herself, the more she will tend to feel victimized and try to avoid responsibility for her choices.

Some women feel better in a paradoxical way if they think of themselves
as bad for having had an abortion. It is more in keeping with other familiar
feelings of unworthiness, and thus, in a strange way, comforting. If feeling
good requires that she sacrifice herself, and having an abortion is seen as
the easy way out, a woman may choose (unconsciously) to feel bad about
herself for having chosen not to sacrifice herself.

Some women characterize themselves as selfish and bad for wanting to
have a baby as well. They feel so bad about their possible choices that they
feel unable to make a decision.

A woman who feels trapped and extremely guilty about her choices
might feel suicidal because she carries debilitating doubts about her own
right to exist.

Many women feel no guilt about abortion. Some will question that and
wonder if they *should* feel guilty. In other words, some of us feel guilty because we don't feel guilty!

Sometimes, guilt can be the energy for the continuation of unacceptable
thoughts.[13] Many women cannot accept the thought of loving and caring
for themselves in the same way they would for another person. This kind
of guilt is rampant among women. Healing the low self-esteem that is at
the root of it is a central part of achieving personal empowerment.

Facing the emotional pain associated with persistent guilt about abortion can heal the personal fears and insecurities that threaten a person's integrity and ability to walk freely in the world. It is also an opportunity to
take a closer look at the broader societal influences on women's self-esteem.

Difficulty Initiating Decisions

In society today, it is still generally expected that men will lead and
women will follow. Even if a woman develops a capacity for decision

making, she might feel she should defer to someone. If we are accustomed to letting others make decisions for us, we could have great difficulty making a decision about a pregnancy.

In addition to fear and confusion about a crisis pregnancy, women might delay making a decision about the pregnancy because of the taboo against initiating action in our lives. This puts us in the position of needing an abortion later in pregnancy than we would have liked.

Other women choose too quickly without fully examining all aspects of their situation.

When women find it difficult to make a decision or initiate action, we experience mental paralysis and generalized anxiety. We believe we are incompetent to make the right decision. The pressure of time heightens the anxiety and may feel overwhelming.

Having Needs Is Normal

The powerful cultural archetype of the self-effacing, self-sacrificing mother is considered a social ideal for women, so many women carry significant guilt for having any needs of their own. Some of us go so far as to deny that we have any needs.

Dependency needs—the desire to rely on another person for physical and emotional nurturing and support—are natural and normal. They do not go away regardless of how well they are denied or repressed.

Since the needs do not disappear and women are encouraged not to be open and direct, as well as being taught not to take our own needs seriously, we sometimes resort to unconsciously manipulating others to get our needs met. The energy of our unmet needs can be perverted into caring for and controlling the lives of others. The popular term for this pattern is *codependency*.

A Word About Codependency

The term *codependency* came into popular usage in the nineteen eighties. Thank goodness interest in it is waning now. It described patterns of taking care of others at one's own expense and of finding self-worth and identity as a caretaker of others. The term originated in the movement to understand and treat alcoholism and alcoholics. It was used to describe the wife of a male alcoholic and her role in enabling her husband's alcoholism and his dependence on her care.

The idea of codependency has been confused with general issues of dependence, which affect the majority of the population. It has been overgeneralized and used to obscure the true nature of emotional power in relationships.

The popularity of the term indicates a growing desire of many people for emotional equality in personal relationships. However, the widespread labeling of people as *codependent* misrepresents an important dynamic in society.

For centuries, women have found self-worth and identity in taking care of others at our own expense. Female existence in male-dominated society is characterized by facilitation and manipulation of the lives of others.

When a person is labeled *codependent*, she is led to believe that something is wrong with her, rather than understanding the historical and social context in which her life and personality unfolds. She might pull back from her natural human urge to be caring because she is afraid of being codependent.

The Value of Caring

Historically, female identity includes learning to care consciously and to differentiate between caring and caretaking. For thousands of years the social role of women has been to take care of others. It has been assumed that women would do this and we have not had much choice in the matter.

While society has depended on women's ability to connect and care for others, being able to separate and be independent—the traditional masculine way—has been considered more important and valuable.

If women are to advance in our personal and collective evolution, we must learn how to choose to care rather than assuming the caretaking role.

Pregnancy can put women in touch with their sense of caring. Considering abortion brings that caring to the level of conscious choice.

When we give ourselves permission not to care some of the time, our choice to be caring takes on more significance. Paradoxically, it is women's newly developing sense of ourselves as autonomous, separate beings that allows us to freely feel our connectedness with others and with All Life.

Woman's choice not to be defined solely by our biological and social role as mother is a moral and ethical position of caring about the quality of relationships, including our relationship to all aspects of ourselves.

The moral position of most women in the abortion decision is neither pro-life nor pro-choice. Those positions were developed in order to establish categories of opposition in patriarchal political battles. They are only partially relevant to the predicament of a pregnant woman because they are based on concepts of fairness and individual rights.

Pregnancy decisions have little to do with fairness or individual rights. They are about the quality of human relationships in the context of specific circumstances. A woman's decision to bring through or turn back a pregnancy stems from her perceptions and judgments about her life situation at a particular time. A pregnancy in another situation might bring her to a different conclusion.

Circumstances change, and people change with them. An attitude that generalizes about the rightness or wrongness of abortion does not speak to the experience at all.

Pregnancy and Self

Barbara Katz Rothman writes in her book, *The Tentative Pregnancy*:

> *In the experience of pregnancy two beings both are, and are not, one. That is an obvious reality, but it is one we continuously deny as we first speak of them as a unit, and then speak of them as separate. The uniqueness of the pregnancy relation eludes our ability to define. We*

have to learn to see, to express, attachment and separation at once. It
is easier to see the shifting balance over time, than to see that all the
while, two are one. [14]

Women do not exist for the sake of others. A woman exists for herself. However, self, which is actually a process rather than a thing, does not exist by itself. Self exists in relation to others and its environment. The development of the emerging self requires evaluating a person's relationship to others and how those relationships define her. This evaluation is crucial with regard to a woman's relationship to a pregnancy or fetus.

Pregnancy is the quintessential relationship. There is no other human life connection on the physical plane that is more intimate or more rooted in relatedness. A woman experiences the fetus and the pregnancy process as parts of herself. What is contained in her body is both otherness and self. The otherness is part of her. All parts of pregnancy are part of her.

An unwanted pregnancy can cause a woman to feel alienated from herself, most dramatically from her body. Spaciness and disorientation characterize the splitting she does in her mind. She finds it difficult to identify with her physical experience and could even feel like it is happening to someone else. She might express this as a sense of being invaded by an alien being. She might speak of *wanting my body back*. (Women having desired pregnancies sometimes feel this way too.)

The split is not simply between self and other. In pregnancy otherness is part of self, psychologically as well as physically. Otherness is not only the fetus; it is the pregnancy process as well.

Woman Versus Fetus?

Barbara Ehrenreich writes: "Today the fetus is viewed almost as a freestanding individual, while women have all but disappeared. Consider the way we have come to visualize a fetus: as a sort of larval angel, suspended against a neutral background. But no fetus—no living fetus—is suspended anywhere, but anchored to the placenta, housed in the womb, and wrapped in the flesh of a living woman." [15]

The idea of woman and fetus as two completely separate beings denies the actual experience of pregnancy. Psychologically it sets the woman against herself. It asks her to treat the fetus as outside of her and different from her own interest.

A woman and a fetus are inextricably joined in pregnancy. *Her* awareness of the experience reflects the dual aspects of the pregnancy process. No one other than an individual pregnant woman knows—unconsciously as well as consciously—the nature of her experience and the meaning of that experience to her and her life situation.

It is a distortion of reality to think of a fetus as abstract and separate from the woman in whom it exists. It is also demeaning to women and disrespectful of the ways of Earth. Reproductive and developmental processes, whether of animals, plants, or minerals of the land, are an intricate relational dance between life, potential life, and death.

An abortion is an act initiated consciously by a woman or spontaneously by her body (a miscarriage) to discontinue the development of a fetus growing inside her—to end fetal life. There is no organized political movement to punish or condemn a woman for spontaneously aborting. Very few people think that when she has a miscarriage she is killing a fetus. We generally accept the power of the female body to turn back developing fetal life.

It is when a woman becomes a conscious agent in the act of abortion that she becomes subject to suspicion and condemnation. Women's active involvement in life-giving matters threatens the entire system under which we live because it challenges male control.

The political push to elevate the fetus to the status of person ultimately reflects the patriarchal fear of women and the creative, feminine aspects of life. It attempts to offset the life-giving power of women by creating another political entity (fetus as person) to act as an agent of domination. It further splits us from ourselves.

Thus, as we assert our personal moral power to say no in pregnancy, some accuse us of being murderers. When we challenge these accusations and search ourselves for answers to troubling questions, solutions come forward that bring with them an expansion of awareness about life, death, and relationships.

Abby

The circumstances of Abby's abortion were not especially unusual. She went to a local abortion clinic and the medical procedure was done during the first trimester of pregnancy. She had not been pregnant before, and she had hoped that her boyfriend, with whom she had been living for several years, would not object to having a baby. He did object though, and apparently had told her early in their relationship that he never wanted to get married or have children.

When I first met Abby, she cried hard about wanting a baby. She was unaware of any other feelings, and felt utterly powerless and victimized. She was accustomed to pleasing other people and felt guilty for having feelings and needs of her own. She wanted help with the loss of sexual desire since her abortion one year before.

Abby said she would have sex with her boyfriend once a month "just to keep him happy." As time went on she reduced the frequency as much as possible. She felt that her boyfriend, Sam, had forced her to have the abortion because he didn't want to have children or get married. She had never owned the decision herself. She was out of touch and unable to identify any feelings associated with the experience.

Feelings of any kind were unacceptable in Abby's world. Love in her family was conditional and often withdrawn without explanation. Her parents had been physically and emotionally abusive to her, and Abby learned as a child that love was to be earned, but that, no matter what she did, she would never be good enough to deserve it.

Now she suffered from severe anxiety, headaches, depression, sleep disturbances, and eating disorders. She felt confused and deeply ashamed of herself. She questioned her right to be alive. She was prone to fits of anger in which she would feel out of control, triggered by relatively insignificant events in her life, like a disagreement with someone at work. Though most of her symptoms had been going on since adolescence, she had become more aware of them since her abortion and worried that the abortion was making her feel worse.

Abby felt young to me, younger than her twenty-nine years. She carried a deep psychic wounding within her. She trusted no one. She perceived the mildest self-assertion as out of line. She apologized frequently for her thoughts and feelings. Because she measured herself in terms of her mother's negative judgments, she was now facing the task of differentiating her own feelings from her mother's real or imagined feelings, and making the emotional separation necessary to function freely as an adult.

As she worked in therapy Abby was able to feel her anger and hurt towards Sam for not wanting to marry and have a baby, and for not giving her the emotional support she needed at the time of the abortion. She also learned that she had never asked for any help from him because she felt so unworthy of love. She began to see that she did in fact have feelings and that her feelings were valid. In addition, she had never grieved.

Around the time of the second anniversary of her abortion, Abby and I did a short meditation to music in one of our sessions. She had been crying at the beginning of the session, feeling sad about her abortion. I asked her to relax and breathe with the music and focus on her feelings. In her meditation she imagined herself putting a small coffin out to sea. Simple and powerful, the image created in her a feeling of inner peace and a sense of completion.

Abby's pain had to do mainly with feeling unwanted and unloved by her parents. Her sense of being unloved and unlovable was intensified by her rejection of the baby she could have had. Along with the actual loss of the pregnancy, the loss of the baby represented the lost part of herself that had never been loved. She felt empty and enraged, but feelings were unacceptable to her so she denied and repressed them. The rage turned inward and she condemned herself for being selfish and bad for having had an abortion.

So accustomed to letting others tell her what to do and how to feel, she had the abortion because her boyfriend wanted her to. Through our work together it emerged that had she allowed herself to make the decision, she still most likely would have had an abortion because of the instability in her life, both inner and outer. However, because she let her boyfriend make the decision, she suffered from not knowing for sure if she might have continued the pregnancy and had the baby.

Not owning her feelings and not taking responsibility for the decision had left her with a sense of empty powerlessness. Sam was emotionally unavailable for the most part, and Abby did not know how to express her needs. Thus, her one deep desire—to be held in the comfort of loving arms—went unfulfilled.

Abby's anger towards Sam, coupled with her fear of another surprise pregnancy, had numbed her to his sexual advances. Self-condemnation and unexpressed feelings led to flare-ups of panic attacks, frightening dreams, eating binges, and episodes of hysterical crying, all symptoms of childhood abuse. Eventually she left him.

The pregnancy and abortion put Abby in contact with her womanhood. Since she still carried many unmet needs from her childhood, she was sorely unprepared to manage the feelings surrounding her pregnancy and abortion. The pain of Abby's personal process around abortion initiated a new stage in her self-development. Through the process of coming to terms with her abortion she was empowered to begin to take conscious responsibility for her body and her life. She moved out of state and settled in a new city with a new job. She found another therapist and continued to explore the core emotional issues that were preventing her from stepping fully into adulthood. Happily, after a couple of years she met and married a man with whom she had two children.

Abby would be considered a victim of abortion by those who would deny her the right to have one. Because abortion is often seen as an isolated experience in a woman's life, it is easy to credit it with causing all kinds of problems. I would caution against this, and instead urge us to remember the larger context in which the experience takes place. It is important to differentiate between blaming an event for all the difficulties in one's life and understanding the impact of an event on one's life.

An abortion can trigger a crisis in an individual woman, and bring unfinished or wounded aspects of her being to the surface. But while it might expose our shaky sense of self, abortion is not the cause of low self-esteem.

Abortion is a catch point in our culture for fears about the changing status of women, confusion about relationships between women and men, and revelations in the process of healing and self-examination that is bringing issues of sex and sexuality into the open. Women need to be careful not to mimic the culture by using the abortion experience as a convenient dumping ground for feelings about other unresolved aspects of our lives. An abortion might trigger guilt and shame about sexuality and self, but it is not the cause of those feelings.

To find causes for these feelings we must develop a broader, deeper perspective about life as a woman in patriarchal society. At the same time, abortion demands recognition as a pivotal experience.

Just as we must refrain from exaggerating its importance, neither do we want to minimize its impact. For many women the experience brings with it an opening into the depth of their complexity as human beings. It offers the possibility to expand awareness about female existence. It is up to each of us to find the courage to take advantage of the opportunity for personal growth and learning by acknowledging and honoring all aspects of our experience.

For any woman, deciding to have an abortion because someone else wants her to can be a painful lesson in learning to listen to herself and act in her own interest. Learning to act in terms of how she feels and what she needs requires that a woman unlearn much of what she has been taught. It takes time and patience.

If a woman has allowed herself to be pressured to do something she later regrets, she must first honestly admit that this was the case. Then, she can take the necessary steps to develop her capacity to act authoritatively and responsibly in her own best interest.

If we blame other people or circumstances for what happens to us, we give our power over to them and rob ourselves of the opportunity to move into a place of active power in our own lives.

The better we feel about ourselves, the easier it is to act in our own interest. The more we do so, the better we will feel about ourselves. The more we value our feelings, thoughts, and opinions, the more we will be able to establish the kind of life we want for ourselves and those we love.

Abortion Is Life Changing

The oppressive circumstances and ideologies surrounding sexuality and pregnancy crystallize for women at the time of a crisis pregnancy. Along with the pressure of time and the polarization of conflicting feelings, this is what defines the quality of the crisis.

Often the choice for abortion is clear but the feelings about it are not. This is uncomfortable; it is not irrational.

Having an abortion can be a desperate act of survival or a step down the path of personal liberation, or both. A woman's relationship to her personal world, coupled with the conditions of her life, determines the circumstances of her decision making. She is most affected by her perception of what is going on around and inside her at the time a particular pregnancy occurs.

Here are examples of the wide scope of women's circumstances:

- If she is young and experiencing her first pregnancy she may perceive pregnancy as her ticket to happiness, to a new life, or as a way to escape the oppressiveness and insecurity of an unstable home life. Or, she might see it as a threat to her survival and a continuation of a cycle of poverty from which she wants more than anything to extricate herself.

- She may be a single parent struggling to make ends meet, or to free herself from dependence on the welfare system.
- She may be a high school or college student, intent on pursuing her studies.
- She may be a single working woman. She might be a married working woman. She might be a married woman with a child or children devoting her time and energy primarily to their care.
- She may be a lesbian who is confused and frightened about her sexual identity. She may be bisexual.
- She may be mentally or physically ill or disabled.
- She may have been raped by a stranger. She may have been raped by a friend. She may have been raped by a family member.
- She may be in a relationship with a loving, supportive person. She might be in a relationship with someone who treats her badly.
- She may have had a brief sexual encounter under confusing circumstances.
- She may have discovered that the developing fetus is severely damaged or deformed. She might have a living child who requires special care due to special problems.
- She may have a physical condition that would put her life in danger if she were to carry a pregnancy to term.

The main thing that women who choose abortion have in common is that at the time they are pregnant they feel it is best not to continue their pregnancies. The circumstances and reasons are individual. They are personal. And, while it is helpful to understand them, no one should have to justify them.

While there is no way to predict the outcome of decision making about a particular pregnancy, it is possible to understand the circumstances surrounding the decision by examining the factors involved. One important factor is the level of support from others, especially the man involved in the pregnancy. Other contributing factors are a woman's self-esteem and perception of herself, her sense of life purpose, her age and level of maturity, her lifestyle and living situation, her personal belief system, and her emotional stability and coping skills. Still others are her economic status and source of financial support. Also, physical conditions are present for some women that introduce possible medical risk in either full term pregnancy or abortion.

Each of us brings to the crisis our life history, our style of problem solving, and our personal defense system. These factors combine and are given priority within each woman's life and personality in uniquely individual ways.

Personal Morality

Our moral and ethical beliefs guide us in our lives. We are influenced by those around us when we are growing up—parents, teachers, and friends—as well as by religious, educational, and political institutions of the larger society. Often, we are not aware of all the beliefs we carry, and we go through our lives with many assumptions.

A crisis pregnancy might push a woman to define her values and beliefs. This is discouraged in much of society. We are encouraged instead to adopt the values and beliefs of others, especially powerful social institutions such as churches. It is nothing short of revolutionary for a woman to define her own morality.

Personal morality plays itself out in relationships and life decisions. A woman who is in the process of choosing the direction of a pregnancy calls upon what she has learned in her life about what is right and what is wrong.

But what is right in the abstract, or in general, might not fit with what is right for her. She may find that her beliefs are not carved in stone, and that they are evolving all the time. Women who have thought of themselves as pro-life or pro-choice might find that their feelings at the time of a pregnancy take them in unexpected directions.

If a woman's moral beliefs are conflicted or undefined, she could experience emotional pain and confusion around a pregnancy decision. For example, if a woman believes that any pregnancy is meant to be, she might have a personal values crisis when she decides to have an abortion.

Internal conflict about morality points to the need to explore assumptions.

If a woman decides to have an abortion in spite of moral beliefs that pressure her not to, she will need to take some time to pay attention to her inner conflicts and work to understand other beliefs operating within her she may have been unaware of. If we run from our conflicts or try to deny or hide them, they will eventually catch up with us. Compassionate self-examination is gratifying and enriching in the long run because it fosters full participation in life and a clear knowledge of our own true nature.

Support from Others

Life decisions are easier to make when a person has the love and support of family and friends. When we feel loved, respected, and cared for, we feel more confident about doing what we need to do. If our loved ones allow us to freely express what we are feeling and thinking, we are more likely to be able to be clear and honest about our feelings and thoughts.

If those closest to us are judgmental or unsupportive, or if they have their own agendas about how we should lead our lives, we will have a more difficult time dealing with a pregnancy and abortion.

If a woman suspects from past experience that her family and friends will not be supportive, she is likely to hide what she is going through from them.

Sometimes we feel so bad about ourselves that we refuse support from others. We judge ourselves harshly and think others will judge us the same way. We decide in advance that a certain friend or family member will think we are bad or be angry or disappointed with us. We don't give other people a chance to care, because we think we're not worthy.

Sharing the experience with another person can significantly reduce the stress of a crisis pregnancy. However, many women find it difficult or impossible to ask for support. We do not want to bother people or be a burden to them. On the other hand, rarely would we feel bothered or burdened if a friend or sister asked for our help. It's just difficult to ask for that for ourselves.

The support of the man involved in the pregnancy is of crucial importance to most women. A woman needs him to be present and loving, before, during, and after the abortion. He can be helpful by preparing meals, talking about his feelings and thoughts, listening to the woman, and engaging in verbal and physical expressions of affection. If a man supports a woman and is willing to be open, they could experience a deepening and strengthening of the emotional bond between them.

Roger Wade writes: "Whether your relationship is good, bad, or broken up, the main thing to do is to reassure her that you care about her and what is going on. This seems to be something many men would rather leave unsaid. They tend to believe that actions speak louder than words. However, sometimes the message doesn't get across. No matter how good your relationship, or how tuned in you are to each other, say you care out loud. If the relationship is not the best, you can still make it clear that you care about her as a person even if you are not in love with her. If you are into concrete actions take her out to dinner or do some other thing that she really likes." [16]

Unfortunately, many men do not know how to be emotionally supportive. They have received no social conditioning or training in it. The emotional nature of a crisis pregnancy can scare them and they might retreat. The resulting stress on the relationship could be too much to bear. Some relationships are unable to withstand the stress of a crisis pregnancy.

Perception of Self

An unintended or unwanted pregnancy interrupts the daily routines of life. It engenders a heightened sense of self. When it happens, women think, *that happens to other people, not to me.* It is a shock.

If no birth control was used at the time of pregnancy we might describe ourselves as stupid or irresponsible for having engaged in unprotected intercourse. Women who did use birth control sometimes use these self-deprecating characterizations as well. We seem to have very little difficulty blaming and shaming ourselves for events in our lives.

A woman who sees herself as capable of handling whatever comes her way will find it easier to manage the swirl of events and feelings around a crisis pregnancy. Women tangle with many other challenges in their lives. When faced with pregnancy and abortion, we do what we need to do to take care of ourselves.

Anna, a seventy-five-year-old friend of mine, remembering her illegal abortion fifty years earlier, told me how she discovered she was pregnant when her two children were under five years old. Anna had no doubt about her decision to have an abortion, and her husband was supportive. She remembered being frightened about finding someone to perform the illegal medical procedure safely, but she had no emotional conflicts. "I just took care of it," she said, "and have had no regrets since."

Anna's matter-of-fact attitude fifty years after her abortion was indicative of her approach to life in general. She had no patience for dwelling on things in the past. She preferred to approach things practically and had little interest in exploring anything psychologically. It's hard to know how many women are like Anna, but we can safely say that it is unlikely they would be known to helping professionals. Some might accuse Anna of being in denial about her feelings, but I prefer to take her at her word. She reminds us how truly wide the range of experience with abortion is.

A Rite of Passage

Dana was a senior in high school when she came to talk about an abortion she had during the previous school year. Now she found herself thinking about it all the time and feeling bad.

"How can somebody who loves kids have an abortion?" she exclaimed. The upcoming anniversary of her abortion was creating internal pressure. Her graduation from high school was fast approaching. She had entered a major life passage.

Dana loved babies and young children. "I like their brightness, the aura around them, their unconditional acceptance," she said. Babysitting for children brought joy and comfort, but it also brought up Dana's sadness about having an abortion.

Dana was very attached to her mother and received a great deal of love and support from her. It helped when her mom shared the circumstances of her own abortion with Dana as well as her decision to give birth to Dana as a single parent after she was deserted by Dana's father. This information comforted Dana, as much because it confirmed her sense of awe about decision making in pregnancy, as because it helped her feel less alone.

Dana's mother had encouraged her to have an abortion, though she had left the door open for a different decision. Sometimes Dana felt this as support, sometimes as pressure. At her first appointment at the women's clinic, she left without having an abortion because, "I just couldn't do it."

Part of Dana wanted her mother to make the decision for her. Her mother insisted Dana decide for herself. This created tension between them as well as anxiety and fear within Dana as she struggled to gain control of the situation. All her life, her mother had protected and rescued her from difficult situations. Now she had to take care of herself. Part of her welcomed this opportunity, while another, younger part of her resented it.

Now she was having difficulty accepting that she had gone through with having an abortion. She wanted to believe that she would have loved to have had the baby and that her mother and external circumstances were the reason she had chosen an abortion.

She wanted this to be true but she knew it wasn't. As she went back over the story and honestly confronted her feelings, she knew that only she had determined the outcome of her pregnancy.

Now she needed to come to terms with that decision and what it meant about her as a person, especially as an independent person. Separating from the pregnancy came at a time in her life when she was separating from her mother and her childhood self. The process of grieving the loss of the pregnancy was taking place within the context of the loss of her life and identity as a child.

On the day the baby would have been due, Dana went to the newborn nursery at a local hospital. On that particular day no babies were there, which gave her an eerie feeling because "I didn't have mine either." Disappointment and relief combined to lead her to a puzzling question: Had she been trying to make herself feel bad?

I suggested to her that she make some kind of statement to the being that she related to as a baby. She nodded enthusiastically as her eyes filled with tears. At our next meeting she lit a candle and read from portions of her journal, letters she had written to "Dear One."

Dana discovered something surprising as she looked more deeply within herself. She found that she was pleased she was sad and was happy she felt an emotional charge around babies. She said her feelings were "keeping me in a state of emotional turmoil and helping me in my search to know more about my experiences."

Her feelings, though painful, were helping her to know herself. The more she learned about herself, the more she wanted to know.

She faced the fact that while she felt sadness and loss about the baby, she also didn't care about it. This was difficult to admit at first, but one day she suddenly said, "Even if it were God's baby I wouldn't want it!" She remembered that one time when she was pregnant she had thought of suicide because she couldn't imagine having either a baby or an abortion.

Anti-abortion groups picketing the clinic where she went for her abortion had frightened her. Pictures of fetuses with little hands and feet had upset her terribly. The images were imprinted in her mind. One way she was able to work this through was to interview someone from a local anti-abortion group for research for a paper for school.

She wrote about the right-to-lifers and went to pro-choice meetings. She wrote in her journal and talked to friends. She went to support groups for teenage mothers and talked with other young women who had had abortions. She began to make plans for life after high school and to say good-bye emotionally to her mother.

She began to see that life was full of life-and-death decisions, and that life contained a great deal of change and uncertainty. She realized she was escaping responsibility for present decisions by thinking *if only I had had the baby,* every time something turned out differently from the way she wanted.

Dana spent her senior year of high school in a state of growing self-awareness. Her abortion gave her a pivotal focus with which to tackle the formidable task of becoming a separate individual. As she learned about loving and letting go she was able to sympathize with her mother's difficulty in letting go of her, as well as her own tendency to cling to childlike ways of relating.

Dana had the courage to open to her internal questions and insecurities, and was thus able to move into an insightful place of awareness. As she moved into adult awareness she was able to take with her the positive, joyful qualities of her child self. Understanding the pain of her abortion gave her the tools to grasp essential aspects of her life and relationships.

The child self is that aspect of us that is organically connected to the life of the body, the way children are. It is free flowering and free flowing, especially emotionally. This part of us is not at all introspective. It is the part that experiences life spontaneously and without self-consciousness. It is athletic, earthy in a physical sense, instinctive, playful, emotional, sensual, innocently erotic, with a strongly developed sense of the child within.[17] A healthy child self supports us to move in the world in ways that are respectful of our earthly origin.

Dana protected this part of herself as she moved through the darkness of her doubts and fears about having had an abortion. It was the area of herself that she was most comfortable with, and she was able to enlist it to serve her as she dropped into painful places. Personal growth through the abortion experience stands on the shoulders of all the growth and development a person has achieved up to that point. The strength of Dana's child self supported her to move into her sense of herself as an adult. Her pregnancy and her choice to have an abortion sowed the seeds of personal growth. She proceeded naturally through all the stages of healing: she faced the crisis, fell apart, reached out for support, recognized and clarified her feelings and beliefs, fully acknowledged what happened, grieved her losses, and moved into acceptance and forgiveness.

History and Women's Lives

The system of patriarchy is a historic construct; it has a beginning; it will have an end.

—GERDA LERNER, *THE CREATION OF PATRIARCHY*

W E USUALLY THINK OF ABORTION AND OTHER REPRODUC-
tive issues as only or mainly personal, and, while they are personal for sure, it can be immensely helpful to have a deeper, broader
perspective rooted in an understanding of how issues arise and become
political and contentious in the larger community. When we add a historical perspective to our personal experience, we create the kind of
knowing that relieves us of undue private burdens and helps us understand that each of us is part of the larger collective of human experience.

History is knowledge about the movement of life in time and space. A
sense of history and an understanding of social and economic relations in
society can aid us in understanding the place of abortion in modern life
and how it affects our current thinking, consciously and unconsciously.

Our own individual psychological experience makes more sense when it rests on an understanding of historical and social realities.

The psychology of abortion is rooted in historical realities that surround and are contained within individual human beings. In patriarchy, women's ability to create life has been used against us to keep us subservient to men and overwhelmed with responsibility for others, especially children. This is the historical context that shapes women's experiences with abortion.

The assertion of women as individuals in their own right, apart from their reproductive function, is a relatively new development in history. It could signal a turning point for all humanity with regard to the value of the individual. This benefits men as well as women because it lays the foundation for the full flowering of humanity without regard for rigid, artificial, gender-bound restrictions. The availability of abortion is crucial to this process.

Abortion at this time in history is double aspected. It is about the reproduction of life *and* the power of women.

Up to this time, human evolution has required the subordination of women and limiting women's lives to sexual and reproductive function. It is no longer necessary for the survival of our human species for the sexes to be divided unequally. The liberation of women from the limitations of our reproductive role is necessary for the advancement of human evolution.

We are in the early gestational stages of this change. Our time is preparing the ground for the transformation of society from one of domination and subordination to one of equality and the flowering of creativity. How will we spread the seeds? In what direction will we take our development? How will we know which way to go?

The historical shift from domination, war, and fear, to equality, peace, and love will occur over centuries. It is unlikely we will see it in our lifetimes. Our responsibility is to allow it to happen for those in future generations by paying attention to what can be changed now and by taking responsibility for our lives.[18]

Social, political, and personal conflicts about abortion have their roots in the contradictions of present day reality and reflect the historical shift occurring now. The crises so many of us confront about our identity and the direction of our lives manifest on a personal level this monumental historical, societal change.

When we face our choices in pregnancy, we confront our individuality and possibilities for conducting our lives beyond the ways dictated by historically established sex roles. Thus, for many women, having an abortion is a combination of moving beyond the restrictions of patriarchy while surviving within them. Emotional conflict and confusion reflect thousands of years of women's subordination in addition to current personal conditions.

Women have been in the center of history equally with men, but record keeping has included women only marginally. The chronicling of history has been subsumed under patriarchy. As a result, instead of placing women in the center of human experience along with men, we have been relegated to the sidelines.

The individual and collective reality of women has been male centered and male dominated for the past 5,000 or more years. Patriarchal modes of social organization have determined the extent to which women have been able to assert our needs and control our destinies. The organization of sexual relationships, birth patterns, and abortion has been regulated by the economic and population needs of those who ruled particular societies.

The central place of women in pregnancy, birth, and abortion has been taken for granted at best, and completely denied at worst. The intrinsic power of women contained within these experiences threatens a power structure that depends upon a belief in the superiority of men and the unequal division of society into economic classes.

Male centered and male dominated modes of thinking function to maintain social and economic forms that wield the power of a small number of men over women, children, and most other men. These systems of class division and domination have been the prevailing modes of societal organization for the same period of time. They operate in tandem with patriarchy.

Social change in the nineteenth and twentieth centuries made the role of women in history more visible. As women have become aware of the re-

strictions in our lives, we have examined how to change the way we participate in society.

Our search, then, becomes a search for the history of the patriarchal system. To give the system of male dominance historicity and to assert that
its functions and manifestations change over time is to break sharply with
the handed-down tradition. This tradition has mystified patriarchy by making it ahistoric, eternal, invisible, and unchanging. But it is precisely due to
changes in the social and educational opportunities available to women
that in the nineteenth and twentieth centuries large numbers of women finally became capable of critically evaluating the process by which we have
helped to create a system and maintain it. We are only now able to create a
consciousness which can emancipate women. This consciousness can also
liberate men from the unwanted and undesired consequences of the system
of male dominance. [19]

The basis for what is normal and natural for women has been changing
noticeably for the last 150 years. Marriage and motherhood are no longer
assumed to be the main or only acceptable life activities for women. Large
numbers of women have entered the work force to stay, as primary wage
earners. Many women see themselves identified with their work as well as
with their roles as wives and mothers.

The social forms necessary to support this change, like high quality child
care, flexible work hours, nonexploitive working conditions, guaranteed
housing and health care, and equal, cooperative personal relationships,
have not yet materialized on a mass scale. Thus, it is necessary for women
to seek maximum protection and control over their lives. This is the context
in which legal abortion has become a public necessity.[20]

The free choice of abortion can feel threatening to women who feel dependent on men because they perceive it as letting men off the hook, ab-
solving them of their traditional responsibility to support and protect
women and children. A woman who feels this way might fear being forced
to have an abortion when she doesn't want to have one. Traditional marriage and motherhood might seem attractive to a woman for whom there
are no other options for safety and security. This could have been one of

the reasons women consented to subordination in the family and society thousands of years ago. If no other options seem available or attractive, a woman might feel she has a right to be protected and supported by a man.

With the rise of feminist consciousness, we see that family forms headed by men result from the evolution of humanity. They are not the only natural forms. They are merely functional from the point of view of history and the needs of an evolving society. They are not the only forms possible, nor are they necessary any longer.

Human society is moving in the direction of fundamental reorganization. Abortion, with all its conflicts for individuals and societies, represents the times in which we live. It leads us into a discussion of woman's role in society, relationships between women and men, the structure of the family, the value of children, sex and sexuality, individual identity, and the relationship between humans and nature.

The organization of society into stratified economic classes with one class controlling how all of its members live has alienated human society from the natural world.

> Patriarchal man created—out of a mixture of sexual and affective frustration, blind need, physical force, ignorance, and intelligence split from its emotional grounding, a system which turned against woman her own organic nature, the source of her awe and her original powers.[21]

Abortion links us back to the natural world and especially to its cycles of birth and death. The natural power of women to give birth and to transform life continues to be a central part of human life in spite of the patriarchy's attempts to demote it to secondary status.

We have reached a time in history when the reproduction of our species is not as crucial to our survival as it has been in the past. Human society possesses the knowledge and technological ability to feed and care for all people. Infant and maternal mortality—the rate at which babies and young children and their mothers die—is manageable.

Since more people are surviving childhood and living longer, it is no longer necessary for women to concentrate our energies on procreation. As we free ourselves from subservience in our role as reproducers, the profound nature of reproduction and of birth and death is revealed.

Just as the ancients revered the ability of women to make life from life, we now look forward to a time when we respect the Cycles of Life and incorporate them into our consciousness for individual and collective creative purposes.

This change will affect all of society and all of our personal and work relationships. Some of the guidance for this change comes from knowing about Goddess worship of ancient times. Feminist historians, anthropologists, and philosophers in the twentieth century discovered much that shows how pre-patriarchal societies operated in terms of the equality of the sexes. The life-giving function of women occupied a central place in these societies. Spiritual forms reflected society's awe and respect towards Creation and the life cycles.

The current revival of nature religions in techno-industrialized countries like the United States reflects a desire to reconnect with the Earth and the natural world. Along with women's search for positive identity, concern about the environment and a sense of planetary unity has spurred interest in the spirituality of the Earth.

Ancient peoples knew this spirituality well. They did not experience themselves as separate from Nature. They developed spiritual forms to live in synchrony with Earth's cycles. Their physical survival depended on living in balance with Nature—something many people today are discovering is still necessary. The value of knowing about the time before patriarchy lies in the knowledge that there will be a time after it.

Before Patriarchy

Patriarchal society has been in existence for so long it's difficult to imagine a society that is not patriarchal. The same goes for society organized along economic class lines. Is anything else possible? What would it look like if one group or individual did not dominate another?

Before patriarchy, human life was organized in small groups. The tasks of living were shared among women and men. Humans at that time were learning to survive physically. Differences between female and male did not determine status or value. One sex was not valued over the other. One did not dominate the other.

Early human societies centered on the activities of women. Women's main activities were in areas of agriculture and the "domestic arts." Their role was fundamental to the organizing and civilizing of human society, yet this is often overlooked in historical accounts.[22]

Early civilizations worshipped the power of women to bring forth life. Woman's body was seen as an extension of Mother Earth and treated with the same reverence and respect given to the planet and its natural cycles. Goddess worship developed out of connection with the Earth and the female life creating process.

The Great Goddess

The Great Goddess or Mother Goddess was an all-knowing, all-loving, all-giving, all-taking power of Life. She was responsive to the needs of human beings as long as her needs and desires were respected.

The Great Goddess could be seen in every aspect of the world. All the rivers, mountains, plains, valleys, trees, rocks, flowers, and animals were aspects of her. She was the source of all nourishment and all life. She transformed life to death and back to life again. All healing happened with and through her.

Anything in Life that was out of balance could be set right by appealing to the wisdom of the Great Goddess. Early people learned to recognize the healing power of plants and the spiritual essence of All Life. Through close observation over time the wisdom of this was applied to human life. Humans, the Goddess, and all living creatures shared the adventure of Life on Earth.

She was a power but a nurturing one. She rebuilt what she destroyed. She transformed what died with her. The Great Goddess was a nurturing mother and all were part of her.

When a living creature died, the Great Mother reabsorbed it into her embrace. Death was part of Life. It was commonplace. Someone or something was always dying. It was part of daily life. Simultaneously life recreated itself through the power of the Great Mother. Someone or something was always being born.

Through simple observation, early people knew that birth and death cycled through the female. The male's involvement was important but different, not as central when it came to the creation of sustainable life. Men worshipped the Great Goddess and saw her power reflected in the bodies of women giving birth and feeding infants with their bodies.

Women and men together wanted to be aligned with the Goddess to secure safety and comfort. Knowledge of the seasons provided information about agriculture. Watching the stars and the moon and the relationship of the sun to the Earth gave ancient people knowledge of the seasons.

"There was unity among earth and the stars, humans and nature, birth and death, all of which were embodied in the Great Goddess..." [23]

Knowledge also developed about curative medicinal plants. Women gathered the plants and treated them to create medicines for everyone. Women and men developed their knowledge side by side. "Woman, in pre-civilized society, must have been man's equal and may well have felt herself to be his superior." [24]

Woman's life-giving process placed her in the home, bearing and caring for children. Her part in the early division of labor was essential to early human development. Eventually her position became subordinate but it didn't start out that way.

The Rise of Patriarchy

It took a long time to establish male dominance as an institutionalized system. Patriarchy evolved over a period of 2,500 years, approximately

between 3100 and 600 BC. It's likely that the original agreement to subordinate woman's position in society occurred with the cooperation of
women for the benefit of society as a whole. No one could have foreseen
the consequences.[25]

As society developed, the subordination and oppression of women became the foundation of class societies, from slavery to feudalism to present
day capitalism. Early societies learned that economic power could be gained
and maintained by controlling sexual behavior and, through that, the lineage
of families. Economic power and the survival of ancient societies depended
upon keeping population rates manageable. Thus, it became a necessity of
survival to control female sexuality and procreation. This meant that sometimes abortion was acceptable and permitted, sometimes not.

The patriarchal family provided the structure for the first institutionalized class system. Women were divided in class society but sexual exploitation of women existed for women in all classes. Men were defined by their
position in the economic hierarchy. Women were defined by their relationships to men. Men owned the reproductive capacity of women.

Slavery as a system began with the enslavement of women. In every slave
society in history, female slavery has been enforced by rape, pregnancy, and
the psychological attachment of women to their children. This is as true
for the enslavement of Africans in the United States in the seventeenth,
eighteenth, and nineteenth centuries as it is for slavery three thousand years
ago in Mesopotamia and Greece.

If we keep in mind that to move human society towards economic abundance all relationships have had to have the economic survival of the ruling
elites as their primary focus, we can see why the control of women's sexuality has been a centerpiece of "civilization." The bedrock of class societies
consisted of the subordination of women to men. Women have been divided through the centuries according to class, race, and nationality. But
in each class, race, and nationality women have been subordinate to men.

There are some who would argue that the development of patriarchy
was a 5,000-year-long detour.[26] I can't go along with that line of thinking

because I don't think it serves the truth of our understanding or the progress of society. Whether we like it or not, or think it unfair, history developed the way it did for reasons that had to do primarily with the survival of the species. I am grateful that we live in a time when the basis for inequality in society is being questioned and changed. I don't doubt that the root of this is that the historically derived possibility of economic life not based on exploitation may be within reach in the foreseeable future.

The Exile of the Goddess

As patriarchy and class society became entrenched in the organization of human life, the central position of women in society was pushed aside. Women's sexuality as well as women themselves became defined by and confined to their role in the bearing and rearing of children. Women's creative powers were minimized and their power to determine the direction of their lives and the life of society was forced underground.

One of the main ways to enforce the devaluation of women was to erase the existence of a divine feminine power. As patriarchal society developed and established itself, the sacred stories and symbols of the Goddess were altered to fit the new system and change the way people perceived reality.

This was powerfully done in the Bible. For example, the serpent, symbol of prophetic wisdom, was one of the chief symbols of the Goddess. In the Bible, it became a symbol of evil. Eve's position in creation is seen as less than Adam's because she was receptive to the serpent and the tree of knowledge. The divine energy that was believed to have created Adam and Eve was the male god Yahweh, later known as Jehovah. His presence and power completely took over from the creation goddesses of earlier times.[27]

Through the ideas expressed in the Bible, procreativity is transferred from female to male. The male seed becomes the central factor in procreation. Mothers all but disappear.

Patriarchy, Class, and Sexuality

As patriarchy became established, systems of class rule arose. Property was passed from father to son, and women were excluded from social and economic control. The subservience of women served the systems of class rule based on ownership of property. Women became the property of men, and sexual relations became immersed in the consciousness of possessiveness.

Much of our thinking about sexual relationships is based on the concept of possession. Capitalism, the current form of class society, bases all its relationships on ownership or non-ownership of property. Those who own property, especially income producing property, have far more power in society than those who do not.

Inequality of personal power in intimate relationships creates fear and competition. This can be completely overcome only by changing fundamental relationships in society. Ideas about possession will change as people learn to live cooperatively in society. This will require a fundamental shift away from capitalism and from property as the standard measure of human worth.

In personal relationships, individuals become caught up in the contradictions between possessing another person and loving that person unconditionally. It's not possible to do both because possession of another person implies power and control over that person. Unconditional love, intimacy, and the free flow of sexual energy occur only when people are free to express themselves and when there is equality and mutual respect between them. Possession has no place in relationships that are truly loving.

Sexuality is the energy of creating and expressing love. It generates possibilities for loving expression and genuine caring, but becomes distorted and repressed by societal barriers and structures that limit it to the needs of patriarchy and class society.

The rules about how sexual relationships must be conducted are based primarily on the control of sexual behavior. The rules developed over thousands of years as patriarchy became established. Organized religions, including Judaism, Islam, and Christianity, claimed the rules were the direct result of divine will. The rules were actually man-made, the product of the needs of society at different points in history. Buddhism and Hinduism reflect these needs as well. Human society needed to move forward to develop its life base and resources. The life organization that was chosen reflected the needs of the times.

Forms of marriage and ways of managing families were tied to society's need that inheritance and property remain in the hands of those who controlled society economically. The division of women into categories of *respectable* and *unrespectable* (*good girl* and *bad girl*) was based on their relationships to men who were or were not propertied. It served the interests of those who owned and controlled the wealth and property.

It was expected that a woman would be attached to a man. If she were not, she risked going without the protection of society and being labeled bad or evil.

The Sexual Double Standard

Marriage, as it has evolved over the centuries, was closely tied to the economic structures and needs of society. Until the last half of the twentieth century, marriage was viewed as the union of a woman and a man with the man in a position of dominance. The marriage "partnership" was an agreement for people to fulfill their social roles according to their gender and for the woman to be subordinate.

A woman's sexuality was owned by her husband in marriage. Part of her obligation was to provide him with sexual services and children, especially sons. He did not have the same obligation to her. His sexuality was considered his own and how he chose to express it was his own business. With very few exceptions, customs about sexual fidelity were not enforced for men. As monogamous marriage and the family became the basic form of organization for society, women who were outside of the system were given little recognition or protection.

As pre-patriarchy moved into patriarchy and matrilineal family bonds became patrilineal, women lost their status in human society. Frederick Engels referred to it as "the world historic defeat of the female sex."[28]

The role of women in the procreation and maintenance of life was no longer to benefit society as a whole, but rather for the individual male "head of household." Her sexuality was valid only in terms of her economic role in the family. It was owned by her husband and regulated by the laws of society. Though laws differed from one society to another and one historical period to another, they all served to restrict and oppress women.

Preserving Female Experience

Though historically necessary, subordination and oppression are never comfortable for those being subordinated and oppressed. When patriarchy and class society evolved, those who were oppressed resisted. While women participated in their own oppression, they also developed ways to preserve and protect female experience.

Over the centuries, side by side with the rules and restrictions of patriarchy and class society, communities of women existed that carried on the ancient traditions of earth wisdom, maintained family life, and regulated pregnancy according to their own and their families' needs. Against great odds, some women were able to become educated and express their ideas and creativity.

The history of daily life for most civilizations is the history of work, family relationships, and creative expression. These aspects of Life have not been given much value or documentation because they do not revolve around the acquisition of property and power. The significance of the presence of women has rarely been noted.

Abortion and Patriarchal Law

For most of patriarchy's history women have been property, either of individual men or of the state. As patriarchal law developed, it treated the "fruit of the womb" as property as well. Laws in ancient Mesopotamia, Assyria, and Babylonia reflected the ways in which the patriarchal rulers needed to control women's sexuality, marriage, and population.

When a woman was pregnant, the fetus was considered the property of her husband. Anyone harming her or her pregnancy had harmed the property of her husband and was obliged to receive punishment according to the laws of the day. As the laws changed over the centuries, it became a serious act against the state for a woman to make the decision to abort a pregnancy. However, infanticide and abortion were practiced in many societies at different times for different reasons, but decisions about abortion and infanticide were usually made by men. Often the objects of infanticide were daughters, since male children were more valued. Eventually, the laws controlling women's sexuality moved from the husband's control to the state's control.

In the Roman Empire, regulation of abortion was for the protection of fathers not fetuses. A wife who obtained an abortion without her husband's consent was subject to exile. Abortion was not considered murder. In Ancient Greece, opinion was divided between Plato and Aristotle on one hand, advocating abortion in certain circumstances, and Hippocrates on the other, opposing it.

Little is known about what women thought or did.

As the patriarchal church gained power, papal decrees contradicted each other in an effort to come to terms with the needs of the church to control pregnancy and the behavior of women. Eventually, both abortion and contraception became sins against marriage and God.

Patriarchal religions and governments have made it appear that their beliefs about women, sex, and pregnancy were universal truths. In the nineteenth century, economic and social changes made it possible for women to see the possibility for survival outside of marriage. Movements for women's equality formed and challenged many of the so-called universal truths of patriarchy.

Women's efforts to assert themselves as individuals have greatly influenced the redefinition and reclaiming of womanhood, personhood, and motherhood. In the twentieth century, this effort took shape as an ongoing struggle to establish political and personal power in society. A significant part of the modern women's liberation movement has been focused around legitimizing women's sexuality, birth control, and abortion.

The United States

During the nineteenth century in the United States, white women of the upper and middle classes were expected to confine themselves to activities related to maternity and domesticity. They were not to see themselves or be seen as sexual, nor were they to assert themselves outside their roles as wives and mothers. Tight corsets, which cut off their breathing and made movement difficult, hid their bodily functions and natural body shapes.

The women of the working class were never privileged enough to enjoy the imposed fragility of their upper class sisters. They focused on basic survival. Having little or no control over pregnancy, they would often resort to desperate means to control their fertility.

Throughout history, the absence of access to birth control guaranteed that most women would give birth to many children. A high percentage of children of all classes failed to reach adulthood, succumbing to disease and malnutrition.

In the eighteenth and nineteenth centuries in the United States, a cult of motherhood developed to stem the tide of emerging personhood. This was an attempt to revere motherhood and make sure women didn't think of themselves as good for anything else. Idealized in the home while confined to marriage and childbearing, women were restricted by the cult of motherhood as it supposedly protected them.

Some nineteenth century feminists opposed abortion because it threatened the social status of women. The mostly middle class, white leadership of the women's movement thought abortion represented the misfortune and inferior morality of working class women and prostitutes.

Thus, feminists of the nineteenth and early twentieth centuries were unable and unwilling to advocate for legalized abortion. Perhaps the complexity of the issues overwhelmed their good intentions and caused them to do unintentional harm.

Abortion was and still is associated with sex apart from procreation—sex for its own sake. Sexual freedom was not necessarily appealing to early feminists because they viewed it as license for men to prey upon women. Their cry for "voluntary motherhood" in the nineteenth century feminist movement was a call for women to protect themselves from having sex forced upon them by their husbands. Between 1800 and 1900 the birth rate among white, middle class women dropped dramatically and the incidence of abortion rose.[29]

The cult of motherhood was more fiction than fact for the women of the working class. With the onset of industrialization, women worked in low paying jobs along with their husbands and children. They bore the double burden of jobs outside the home and responsibility for the care of husband, home, and children. The occurrence of many pregnancies sapped them of their energy and shortened their lives.

African women and their descendants in the United States fared worse than anyone. Captured and sold into slavery, they were subjected not only to the backbreaking toil of slave life, but also to the sexual whims of masters who raped them and stole their children. Some slave women chose to have clandestine abortions to save their potential children from the violence and oppressive suffering of slavery.[30]

African-American women have had to put up with racist governmental policies about eugenics and panic among whites about "race suicide." Throughout the history of the United States social policies about women's health care, birth control, and abortion have been engineered around attitudes that promote beliefs about who should or should not reproduce based on class and race.[31]

Abortion has been a primary method of birth control throughout history. Women healers created methods of abortion that included herbal potions as well as mechanical means. They include teas made from common plants like marjoram, thyme, parsley, and lavender, and unusual ones like the root of the worm fern. Women have gone so far as to drink turpentine, castor oil, tansy tea, horseradish, ginger, bluing, Epsom salts, ammonia, mustard, and other substances. Some remedies worked as abortifacients, but many poisonous substances would as likely kill or maim the pregnant woman.[32]

During the nineteenth century in the United States, in state after state, abortion gradually became illegal. Prior to that time, abortion had been outside the concerns of government, left to the private lives of women. Before quickening—the time in pregnancy when the fetus begins to noticeably move in the uterus—there was little concern about a woman's decision to have an abortion.

Side by side with criminalization of abortion, came laws about compulsory sterilization for those deemed unfit to reproduce. Beginning in the 1870s and reaching its peak in the 1920s, these laws, propagated by the eugenics movement, were focused on both population control and the sexual control of women. The women who were targeted were almost always poor and politically powerless. Biological fitness was always associated with social class.

Legal Abortion in the United States

Between 1967 and 1972, beginning with Colorado, several states liberalized their abortion laws, though the laws remained restrictive and it was still difficult for most women to obtain abortions. In 1970, following Hawaii's lead, New York, Alaska, and Washington repealed their restrictive abortion laws.

On January 22, 1973, the United States Supreme Court handed down a decision that would become a focal point of legal and political struggles about women's reproductive rights. The *Roe v. Wade* decision made abortion legal throughout the country.

Prior to the 1973 Supreme Court decision, some physicians put their lives and careers on the line to challenge restrictive laws. The growing

women's liberation movement put abortion rights in the center of its struggle for women's freedom.

Women were gaining awareness of the need to know more about their
bodies and control their health care. As more women obtained illegal abortions in the twenty years preceding *Roe v. Wade*, pressure mounted for legalization. The laws against abortion were simply not enforceable any
longer. Population control advocates, more politically powerful than the
feminist movement, supported legalized abortion as a way to regain social
stability. Advocates of children's rights, the right of a child to be wanted,
were also active. Still, a woman's right to control pregnancy was not given
high priority or even acknowledged. Rather, laws that stressed the right of
physicians to determine how and when abortions were performed became
more important than ever.

The Medical Model

Roe v. Wade recognized that legal abortion primarily pertained to the
rights of physicians. The justices wrote:

> *The decision vindicates the right of the physician to administer medical
> treatment according to his professional judgment up to the points
> where important state interests provide compelling justifications for
> intervention. Up to these points, the abortion decision in all its aspects
> is inherently, and primarily, a medical decision, and basic responsibility
> for it must rest with the physician.* [33]

The medical profession, through the American Medical Association,
had waged a campaign for more than a century to establish its authority
over women's reproductive health care. From its inception in 1847 until
1970, this campaign included opposition to legalized abortion.[34] Most
likely the AMA position stemmed from an attitude of moral superiority of
physicians over the women they were supposed to serve, and a desire to

control the sexual activity of these women. It is unlikely they believed the embryo had an absolute "right to life."

Sex, contraception, and abortion were deemed unacceptable for "respectable" women. Yet, these white women of the middle class were the targeted clientele for the rising profession of primarily male obstetrician-gynecologists. For medical doctors to establish their hegemony in the area of women's health care they had to wrest authority from midwives, the traditional caregivers. They had to convince people that their technology, pharmacology, and surgical techniques were superior to the traditional approaches of community midwifery.[35]

As the influence of obstetrician-gynecologists grew in the nineteenth century, the idea of pregnancy as a medical condition needing treatment grew as well. Physicians became self-appointed protectors of women. They empowered themselves to assess not only the rights of an embryo's life against a woman's life, but the kind of medical care a woman should receive. Physicians contradicted themselves when they claimed an absolute right to life for the fetus at the same time as they assigned themselves the power to declare some abortions necessary.[36]

When I was working as an abortion counselor and doctor's assistant in the 1970s and 80s it always bothered me that the medical profession made a distinction between therapeutic and elective abortion. The categories make no sense to me. I've never noticed any difference between the urgency or legitimacy of one woman's request and that of another woman. The elective category implies that the request for an abortion is frivolous or unnecessary, and that, in my experience, has never been true.

Labeling an abortion therapeutic or elective was part of the medicalization of abortion. It defined the pregnancy crises of women in terms that made sense only to a disease-oriented medical profession. Pregnant women didn't decide whether their abortions were "medically necessary." Doctors did. Physicians applied their categories of illness to determine the outcome of pregnancies. These categories were often unclear and controversial. They usually included the presence of severe fetal abnormality or conditions that were threatening to the life or health of the pregnant woman. It was often difficult to keep them strictly within a biological framework.

Until relatively recently, our society did not recognize the legitimacy of a woman's feelings about ending a pregnancy. Psychiatric literature, as well as general social attitudes, supported the idea that there was something pathological about a woman who didn't want to be a mother, and that a woman's refusal to take on the role of wife and mother indicated underlying personality problems.

It was assumed that women who had abortions would suffer long-range psychological consequences. This attitude was rooted in Victorian prudery about sex and female sexuality, which reached its high point in the nineteenth century. At that time two different standards of sexual behavior, one for men and one for women, were firmly established. Also at this time, medical doctors began to define and dominate the health concerns of women.

During the 1950s and 1960s, a woman who desired a therapeutic abortion (all others were illegal) would have to petition the review board of a hospital. The board would determine if there was enough evidence to grant her a medically necessary abortion. Women often had to demean themselves and make it appear that they were unfit to continue a pregnancy rather than reveal their simple desire not to.

Eventually, psychiatrists became involved. Some began diagnosing women who wanted abortions as psychotic, hysterical, depressed, neurotic, or guilt-laden. Their reasoning was based on the belief that the main function of a woman was to bear and raise children and considered any woman who did not conform to their belief system as mentally or emotionally disturbed.

A few brave psychiatrists diagnosed any woman who requested help getting an abortion regardless of whether she was "fit." They knew how to manipulate the system to meet the strict qualifications for medically necessary abortions, and did so to help the women. These physicians, along with those who performed illegal abortions, risked their careers and professional reputations to help women. We owe them a great debt. Not too much time passed before the psychiatric establishment changed its position and began to support legal abortion on demand. However, the psychic cost to women of the negative labeling has never been measured.

The distinction between elective and therapeutic abortion, still made by some in the medical profession today, holds no real meaning for women. Whether an abortion is considered therapeutic by the medical profession is irrelevant. Women need their health care providers to listen and respond to their needs without judgment or condescension. Any abortion freely requested by a woman is therapeutic in the most basic sense, since it corrects and heals the life course of that woman. Each woman needs to be supported and respected to determine her own life course.

The Body and Sexuality

*Our bodies are the physical bases from which we move out
into the world; ignorance, uncertainty—even at worst,
shame—about our physical selves create in us an alienation from ourselves that keeps us from being the whole
people that we could be.*

—BOSTON WOMEN'S HEALTH BOOK COLLECTIVE,
OUR BODIES, OURSELVES

IN 1969, THE BOSTON WOMEN'S HEALTH BOOK COLLECTIVE
published the first edition of *Our Bodies, Ourselves*. It was one of the
first books to address the widespread alienation of women from their
bodies, and it suggested that it was possible to be an active player, rather
than a passive observer, in the life of the body.

In the many hours of private counseling sessions with women whose
lives were turned upside down by unexpected pregnancies, I have noticed
the persistent presence of sexual conflicts and confusion about sex. The
charged atmosphere of our time together was marked by embarrassment,
fear, and feelings of being out of control.

The fact that their bodies were central to their current crisis brought out many conflicts and feelings that had to do with much more than abortion. Their pregnancies made them come face to face with their sexuality. Most of the women I talked with were not comfortable with that. They felt alienated from their bodies and unprepared to discuss what was happening to them.

Pregnancy brings a woman's awareness directly to her body and its femaleness. She is forced to focus her on body's processes and on the life of the body. Initially, the bleeding she may have taken for granted each month doesn't come. She misses her period and senses her body rhythm skipping a beat and shifting into new relationship. She might even miss the sight of the blood and long for its return. She could feel a secret excitement about the power of pregnancy.

A pregnancy is a remarkable event. Even if it isn't intended or wanted, elaborate fantasies and joyful feelings may occur. Though these feelings might not continue, they serve an important function. Fantasies create possibilities. It is important to give the fantasies free reign, to release the mind to flow with all that could be, and to develop the possibilities on a mental level in order to maximize the choices on a physical level.

This is easier said than done. A surprise pregnancy can be shocking, and it might not be possible for a woman to get beyond her generalized fear and sense of being out of control. She might believe that because she has decided to have an abortion, she should not enjoy being pregnant.

Pregnancy, for many women, is a dream from childhood, of babies and love, of happiness and security, of fulfillment. However, when it is unwanted, the dream becomes a nightmare. A woman might feel like her body has betrayed her. One woman put it this way in her journal:

> *Pregnant. Containing another life. Female fulfillment? I don't think so. At least not right now. Biological entrapment is more like it. The act of implanting in a hostile host the beginning of a new life unwanted by anyone. What right does this thing have to be growing inside me? What kind of rude invasion is this? How angry I am. How scared, too.* [37]

The desire to be free of pregnancy can be overpowering. She might try to separate from the pregnancy mentally before separating physically, and feel a profound alienation from her body.

"It's like running from yourself, wanting so badly to get away from yourself and wanting that part of you that has been taken over by an alien being to disappear." [38]

The degree to which a woman already feels alienated from her body might heighten the intensity and severity of an unwanted pregnancy. She may feel more split off from herself than usual. Her own body feels like an unsafe and unnatural place to be.

From Nature's point of view, pregnancy is quite unremarkable and ordinary. It occurs in spite of and beyond anyone's idea of it or feelings about it. It is arbitrary and almost careless in its placement and in its outcome. Bodies become pregnant because they can. Spontaneous abortions occur on their own. Some people get pregnant who don't want to be. Others, who want more than anything to become pregnant, are unable to. Pregnancy can seem like a whim of Nature, an expression of Nature's unrefined sensuality and raw, earthy power, its juice. Many women feel a sudden and overwhelming sense of this when faced with an unwanted pregnancy. It can feel foreign because we live in a culture that pretends to be separate from Nature.

Objectification and the Double Standard

The root of our feelings of alienation from our bodies is our society's estrangement from Nature, which is bolstered by the patriarchal mismanagement of women's needs. An expression of our society's estrangement from Nature is the social practice of objectifying women's bodies. Combined with the capitalist practice of treating people as though they were commodities, it is not surprising that we often feel denied our humanity and separated from the bodies in which we live.

To be objectified is to be treated as a thing, an object for use by another. The experience of being objectified is dehumanizing. It causes us to see ourselves as others see us and to lose our connection with ourselves. Sometimes we feel like we don't exist at all. It is frightening and alarming. It is painful.

The objectification and sexualization or desexualization of women's bodies prevents women from developing a grounded, honest sense of self. If we believe our bodies are for the aesthetic or sexual enjoyment of others, we might have difficulty embracing the personal, internal nature of pregnancy.

If a woman feels alienated from her body, she might find that her sense of separation increases when she becomes pregnant. Wanting to get out of her body is an expression of feeling overpowered by the presence of the pregnancy. Cultural messages that tell her that she is supposed to enjoy pregnancy nurture ambivalent feelings about being pregnant.

> *Throughout patriarchal mythology, dream symbolism, theology, language, two ideas flow side by side: one, that the female body is impure, corrupt, the site of discharges, bleedings, dangerous to masculinity, a source of moral and physical contamination, "the devil's gateway." On the other hand, as mother the woman is beneficent, sacred, pure, asexual, nourishing; and the physical potential for motherhood—that same body with its bleedings and mysteries—is her single destiny and justification in life. These two ideas have become deeply internalized in women, even in the most independent of us, those who seem to be leading the freest lives.*[39]

Both women and men in our culture are shamed for being sexual. However, there are significant differences in society's attitudes towards male and female sexuality. Male sexuality is considered to be a natural part of being male. While his sexual activity may not be openly approved, it is expected that a man will act out his sexuality and that it is a basic part of who he is. If this acting out exploits and objectifies women, it is often said that no harm was intended and that it was "all in good fun."

The implication is that men can't be held responsible for their sexual behavior, that they are sexually driven and that they can't help themselves. This is neither biologically nor psychologically true, but too many men behave as though it were true, reacting to cultural messages that "boys will be boys," and a "real man" is domineering and exploitative of women. The idea that men can't control their sexual urges is an ideological justification for the denial and subordination of women's sexuality. It's a disservice to both women and men.

Women absorb and internalize these attitudes. As a result, we often view sex from the man's point of view and believe that his needs are more important than our own. Many women adopt the attitude that they must please men whether or not they please themselves.

A woman's perception of herself in relation to pregnancy and abortion is related to her feelings about herself as a sexual person. Her upbringing and her family's religious and philosophical beliefs influence her sexual attitudes, along with societal behaviors and attitudes.

The main cultural sanction for female sexuality is pregnancy. On an unconscious level, many women believe that getting pregnant justifies the act of sexual intercourse, and so might be relieved about being pregnant. On a conscious level, the feeling could be just the opposite—that pregnancy is the worst thing that could happen. On a conscious level, a woman may still feel relief, but the relief is coupled with anxiety about not really wanting to be pregnant or concern about not being supported by external circumstances. The mix of feelings and perceptions can be terribly convoluted and cause a woman to feel guilt or shame both for wanting or not wanting to be pregnant, and for being pregnant.

These contradictions reflect the unequal power relations between women and men and the sexual disempowerment of women. They are enforced by societally induced shame about sex.

The patriarchal idea that pregnancy is the only reason for a woman to have sex is one of the fundamental social idiocies of patriarchy—the idea that women's sexuality exists only for procreation, except when it is for male pleasure. Thus, sex is "good" for those purposes and "bad" for any other, such as female pleasure.

This, in turn, leads to the peculiar idea that a woman should be forced to have a baby, to "pay," or be punished for having sex and becoming pregnant, by having a baby. This idea shames women for being sexual. The inhumanity of the contradiction becomes glaring when we take it to its logical conclusion—the defining of a baby as a punishment.

If women and men accepted sexual activity as normal, natural, and valuable in and of itself, the incidence of unintended and unwanted pregnancy might be drastically reduced. In most heterosexual sexual situations, the woman's sexuality is subordinated to the man's. This is neither normal, nor natural, nor helpful. If women participated equally with men, they would be able to determine when and under what circumstances intercourse, and therefore pregnancy, would occur.

The confusion around sexual issues makes more sense if one keeps in mind the historically evolving nature of human life and the fact that so much of what we experience as individuals is culturally and socially defined.

Historically, heterosexual sexual relations are modeled on male dominant relationship dynamics. Men are pressured to be sexual and women are pressured not to be. This is a source of conflict and confusion. The pressure on men to initiate sexual interactions, and to control the nature of those interactions, puts women at great risk of unintended pregnancy. Many women are not comfortable with their sexuality and believe that sex is okay only if they are swept away by the man and by the passion of the moment. This mindset, along with difficulty initiating, reduces the chance that birth control will be used consistently. The psychological and relational struggle around this imbalance has been more up front since the legalization of birth control and abortion and other advances in the social equality of women, but the cultural archetypes remain and are tenacious.

Madonna and Whore

In the psyches of individual women in our culture there is a deeply embedded madonna/whore split with regard to female sexual identity. Women identify as good girls and bad girls. This originates in patriarchal culture, which defines female sexuality as good and legitimate within marriage, and bad and illegitimate outside of it.

Within marriage women are desexualized. Outside of marriage we are oversexualized, most notably in prostitution and pornography, but also in fashion circles, on TV, and in magazine ads. Every woman carries within her this self-denying contradiction, which leads to distortion in all our relationships. It makes it impossible to feel whole and complete within ourselves.

The image of the madonna is a virgin mother, a woman who becomes pregnant without sexual intercourse. The concept of the madonna is a contradiction, but it meets the needs of the patriarchal mind, which both reveres and fears the power of female sexuality. It places pregnancy on a lofty plane divorced from sex. Moreover, it denies the connection between pregnancy and active female sexuality, between a woman's body and the energy of sexuality that flows through it.

The female body in the madonna image is a passive vessel in passionless service to pregnancy. Passion and sexual feeling enter the picture only on the side of the whore, the seductress. Like the madonna, the whore's function is to serve the interests of men and male sexuality. Terms that recognize the autonomous existence of female sexuality and its intrinsic value do not exist in patriarchal ideology. It's no wonder we often feel we have lost ourselves.

Fundamentalist Christian teachings revolve around the idea that women are evil and responsible for the fall from grace of all humanity. These ideas are embedded in the collective psyche of modern American society. Individuals carry these concepts consciously and unconsciously. The body of woman is seen as the source of evil and sin, and as dirty. It is also seen as a mystery.

To maintain the social rule of men over women, the fact that man comes from woman has been turned upside down. The stories of the Bible tell us that woman comes from man. If we listen closely, we can hear the Great Goddess laughing.

As a result of the repression of female sexuality, male sexuality has been distorted as well. A man must deny his natural human vulnerabilities if he is to live up to the ideal of the dominant male. He must limit his sexual expression to avenues of control.

Shameful and ambivalent feelings about sex, coupled with many women's belief that it is more important to meet their partner's needs rather than their own, leads to little open, direct communication about sex between women and men. Difficulties in talking about sex come from societal messages that sex is acceptable only if it is done for procreation, and even then it is difficult to talk about.

The so-called sexual revolution of the last forty years or so has brought new, freer concepts into our thinking, but we still hold unconscious beliefs. Traditional concepts of a man as the initiator, the active, dominant one, and a woman as the receiver, the passive one, are no longer assumed to be the only natural sexual way of things. Individual preferences, as well as mutual respect, communication, and openness, are finding their way to being included as part of acceptable and desirable behavior in sexual relationships. Still, sex is confusing because not enough attention has been given to issues of exploitation and personal integrity in sexual relationships.

If people are ashamed about being sexual, they may turn to alcohol or drugs to block their judgment and free their inhibitions. Decisions made in an atmosphere of shame may be impulsive and motivated by guilt or ignorance. The lack of communication about sex and the belief that it is wrong and bad lead to sexual activity that is divorced from the identities of the individuals involved. It is so difficult for so many women to feel good about themselves sexually or in general, that they may fail to act in their own interest in sexual situations.

For most women, the belief that sex is mainly for the man and that they are "bad" if they want to be sexual is so deeply internalized that they are incapable of playing an active role in determining the nature of their sexual experience. This is as true for the "whore" as it is for the "madonna."

Changing attitudes about sex allow us to see new possibilities. Receptivity need not be passivity and active initiation need not be domination.

The sharing and blending of qualities that have been rigidly defined as female or male, combined with equality and mutual respect, sets the stage for the full flowering of human sexual expression.

Saying No, Saying Yes

Tanya was twenty-eight when she joined a post-abortion support group. She'd had three abortions and was seeking support for what she'd gone through.

She described the circumstances of her first abortion as "a particularly painful time." She'd been married at the time and had a two-year-old son. She had not wanted the abortion, but her husband did not want another child. They were divorced shortly thereafter. She'd gone to a hospital and remembered the procedure as a "brutal experience." The doctor and hospital staff treated her coldly.

Tanya's second and third abortions occurred within six months of each other. The pregnancies resulted from birth control method failures. She went to a women's health center for the medical procedures and was treated with caring and respect. The decisions to have those abortions were clear. She was still seeing the man with whom she had become pregnant the second and third times. At the point when she joined the group she was in the process of evaluating the sexual component of their relationship.

Dawn's abortion took place about two years before she joined the support group. She had been twenty-one at the time. She described it as "an incredibly painful experience," both emotionally and spiritually. She joined the group to continue a process of clarification about her feelings that had been going on for some time.

Dawn had been sexually abused as a child by a family member, and had been processing that as well as the abortion. She was interested in how her past sexual experiences were affecting her present relationships.

Sue was eighteen and a senior in high school. Her abortion had taken place one year earlier in a hospital setting under general anesthesia. She wanted to talk with other women about the experience because she couldn't remember much about it. Much of what was discussed in the group was new material for her and she felt young and naive.

In one of our sessions Tanya, Dawn, and Sue had an exchange about sexuality and relationships.

> Tanya: There is a voice in my head that I've never really verbalized, of needing to say no to somebody and not being able to because I felt beaten down. I couldn't say no and I felt kind of raped later. I know that one of the times I got pregnant I didn't really want to have sex. It seems like the kind of relationship pattern that has really affected my pregnancies. Then I realized how many times in a relationship I would equate having sex with getting intimacy and closeness. I wouldn't really want to be having sex, but it would be like I was just so starved for some kind of emotional closeness that I'd give my body away.
>
> Dawn: I had an experience a few weeks ago of being involved in a sexual experience and going into it thinking that it was okay, but then realizing that I didn't want to be having sex, that what I wanted was closeness and intimacy. But my pattern is so ingrained; I equated the two so completely that I'm not even in touch sometimes until after I'm involved. So, I stopped what we were doing and started crying, and I went to such a young, vulnerable place in myself that I wasn't able to tell him what I was experiencing. I was re-experiencing every single time that I had been in a situation where I was having sex and didn't want to. It was like feeling them all at once. I've had vivid memories that have been coming up from early adolescence. I remember a guy telling me that the heavy petting I was doing with boys wasn't enough. I remember just being blown away by that. I had never imagined there was anything else. Suddenly there was this great expectation, so I started being sexual at a very young age. All those years of doing this because I thought that it was what you were supposed to do. There was no pleasure

in it, no intimacy, no closeness. The relationships were completely sexual, and I started to see just how that has pervaded all of my adult relationships. Sexuality, that's how you relate to men, that's how you contact them.

Tanya: It was scary last summer when I told my partner I wouldn't have sex with him anymore. The fear came up for me that, well, of course he's going to leave now because I'm not giving him what he wants, you know...? I'm realizing that rape happens on such a more subtle level than someone throwing you down on the ground.

Sue: I don't know. I mean, I can relate to it, but I keep thinking that I haven't had enough relationships to relate. I was thinking about how many times I had sex with somebody when I really didn't want to. I never really thought about it before.

Tanya: Another thing that I'm just realizing now, having not had sex for a while and learning to say no. I started to finally recognize that there were times when I *did* want to have sex. And I couldn't recognize that in the past. I didn't even really know that. I couldn't feel that. I couldn't allow myself to feel that.

I couldn't allow myself to feel that. How revealing those words are. That women need to say no to sex is an idea currently popular with people on both sides of the sex education political fence. It has been assumed that it is in the interest of women to exert negative control over sex and sexual situations. Whether this is advocated from the point of view of psychological and physical health or moral purity, the message is still the same—disapproval for active female sexuality.

While saying no is often a step towards empowerment, it falls short of real freedom. Women need to be free to say yes, to act affirmatively about our sexual desire.

Sexual relationships between women and men that take place within male sexual definitions and dominance place women in a defensive position.

Tanya had been so busy tolerating sex imposed on her that she was not aware of her own sexual desires. The coercion and dominance of the man was assumed.

True intimacy is not possible in situations of dominance, subordination, and inequality. When one person has personal power over another person and one person gives her power away, it is not possible to achieve enough safety to share vulnerabilities freely and honestly.

Intimate sexual expression often becomes distorted in situations of unequal personal power. As we turn to face each other we also turn away. The urge to be sexually expressive may be present and strong, but ambiguity and confusion causes us to keep one foot in and one foot out of our experience.

People need to look each other in the eye when they have sex, and talk with one another before, during, and after sexual activity. In this way we learn to reclaim our sexuality. We learn to engage our sexuality as a celebration of life and the energy of life that courses through our bodies and defines our humanness.

As heterosexual women get in touch with their own sexual feelings instead of always responding to those of men, they can gain greater awareness of their personal power and authority in sexual situations. Sex becomes more about giving and receiving rather than taking and being taken. It is an expression of the joy of self rather than a repetitive mimicking of procreative function. Madonna and whore cease to exist, replaced by woman as whole sexual person.

Sexual Violence and Abuse

There is no woman in our culture who has not been sexually abused or threatened with sexual abuse. To be abused means to have one's physical or emotional boundaries violated and to be treated as a thing or object. It might occur through physical encounters, verbal threats, or exposure to media portrayals of other women's stories. It might be subtle or overt.

Along with sexual exploitation and objectification, the threat of sexual violence permeates our way of life. This extends into emotional coercion in sexual relationships. The annihilating quality of abuse experiences such as rape and incest often relegates them to the unconscious mind, far from conscious awareness. A person will deny or minimize them in order to survive.

When a pregnancy is felt as a boundary violation, it might bring to the surface other violations that have been denied or buried in the subconscious mind. An abortion can act as a catalyst for uncovering and healing earlier traumas of sexual abuse.

The shock of the pregnancy, and feelings of being trapped and out of control, combined with loss of self, help women to retrieve lost memories of abuse. The body, through the nervous system, re-experiences the earlier traumas and sends its messages to our awareness.

A Healing

A twenty-five-year-old woman who had been brutally raped at the age of thirteen was able to begin healing after she experienced two pregnancies within six months. Though the assault had occurred twelve years earlier, Gayla was unable to face the horror of the experience until the shock of new violations presented her with the opportunity to conduct herself differently.

An intelligent and sensitive young woman, Gayla functioned well in every area of her life except her relationships with men. There she maintained a thirteen-year-old's naiveté and was unable to stop men from treating her badly.

The rape had damaged her ability to make choices and to be in control of her life. It had crippled her ability to feel safe in her own body. She had trusted and looked up to the man who raped her. She felt the rape was her fault. Her self-esteem was shattered.

Each of her two pregnancies occurred in spite of her use of birth control. Each time she grappled with her desire to have children and with the feeling that her body was out of control. She decided to have abortions because her life was not what she wanted it to be to bring a child into the world.

The abortions were painful, physically and emotionally. She was flooded with relief when they were over, relief that she was no longer pregnant. She decided to take a break from sexual relationships to take a look at herself and her life.

Gayla began to realize that the rape had left her feeling powerless to make choices in her personal relationships. Her feeling of taking control of her life by having the abortions stood in stark contrast to the way she felt about the rape.

Slowly she began to shed the numbness of her denial. Carefully she explored painful feelings of vulnerability, including an almost bottomless pit of fear. She got angry. Gayla's anger allowed her to have a clearer sense of her personal boundaries, physically and emotionally. The wounding that had occurred so long ago began to heal.

For some women, the abortion medical procedure triggers memories of sexual assault or abuse. Internal pelvic exams and medical instruments might feel invasive and threatening.

It's a good idea to be thoroughly prepared with information and emotional support before undergoing an abortion. Counseling at the time of an abortion or at any time afterwards provides a woman with the opportunity to discuss her questions and concerns about her body, sexuality, and relationships. It allows her to explore the parameters of her identity, her fears, and the changing possibilities of her definition of herself.

The specific circumstances of crisis pregnancy make women feel vulnerable. Uncovering the multifaceted layers of denial is a central part of healing the pain of experiences that turn on shame and guilt, in which a person harbors a great deal of fear. Though it's not easy, dealing with the confusion of crisis pregnancy in a manner that is honest and true to the feelings involved can help a woman return to her body and herself.

"I Think I Might Be Pregnant"

Beth, a seventeen-year-old young woman, came into the clinic requesting a pregnancy test. She said she thought she might be eight weeks pregnant and that she would like to have an abortion.

Not surprisingly, her urine test turned out to be positive. Next was a preliminary pelvic exam by one of the doctors to estimate the length of pregnancy. This is a routine procedure, especially for teenagers, who tend to have irregular periods and sometimes have more difficulty facing the reality of pregnancy.

When the doctor positioned her fingers inside the young woman's vagina to feel her cervix a strange, semi-alarmed look crossed her face. Trying hard not to scare her young patient, she slowly and deliberately removed her hand, and then her exam glove, helped Beth to sit up, and began to speak.

"Your cervix is effaced. That means you are in the early stages of labor. I can feel the baby's head pushing against your cervix. In my opinion you are going to deliver within the next week or so."

The doctor's estimate of length of pregnancy was 32 weeks. Term is 40 weeks. Estimates of length of pregnancy by pelvic exam are usually accurate give or take two weeks.

Beth was in a daze. My heart pounded and my mind raced as I searched for ways to help her. I had no doubt that she was mentally competent. When I talked with her before the exam, she had been no different from other teens. What was different in her case was that she had managed to ignore the changes in her body during the approximately seven months of her pregnancy.

She had closed her mind and pushed away the reality of the pregnancy. She had told herself she was "just getting fat." Her mind had just opened up enough to let in the possibility that she "might be about eight weeks pregnant."

I asked Beth whether she had experienced any of the symptoms of early pregnancy several months before. She vaguely remembered having been fatigued and nauseated, but had decided at the time that she "just had the flu." She had not had a menstrual period in seven months. It was not clear how she rationalized this, but somehow she had put it aside in her mind.

I had to cover a lot of ground with Beth in a very short amount of time. Not only did I have to break the news to her that she was too far along in pregnancy to have an abortion, I had to support her to let in the reality of the imminent delivery of her premature baby.

Like many teenagers, she focused on how to tell her mother. "My mother will kill me," she said. There was no time to talk about her relationship with the man involved in the pregnancy or her sexual history and feelings about the circumstances of the pregnancy. We could not talk about contraception or her personal moral and spiritual beliefs. She was so stunned that she could barely let in the information I was giving her about her immediate medical needs.

I learned a lot from Beth about the power of psychological denial—how a person can believe anything she wants or needs to believe regardless of evidence to the contrary. She showed me one of the more tragic possible outcomes of the difficulty some women have with sex and pregnancy.

An unwanted pregnancy can be an outrageous and profound psychic and physical boundary violation. Shock about being pregnant, combined with naiveté, ignorance, and shame about sexuality, can cause a woman to completely deny the reality of a pregnancy.

Psychological denial is the process of unconscious lying to oneself. It is complicated to deal with because it operates outside of conscious awareness. We act out an unconscious intention to protect ourselves from threatening information. We mentally detach from our emotions.

The degree of denial that women experience around crisis pregnancy is directly proportionate to the level of their fear. The fear may be about any number of things:

- fear of being judged
- fear of asserting herself

- fear of making the wrong decision
- fear of losing the love of family and friends
- fear of being abandoned by her boyfriend
- fear of being "found out"
- fear of medical things
- fear of dying
- fear of losing fertility

One of the most common phrases spoken by women in pregnancy counseling sessions is, *I didn't think it could happen to me.* Lurking in the shadows of a frightened mind is the idea that it isn't really happening.

Upon finding out she is pregnant, it might take a woman several days to accept the truth of her positive pregnancy test. One woman told me that when she was told she was pregnant she suddenly had "tunnel vision" and was unable to take in what was being said to her. She felt paralyzed, numb, and unable to think clearly about anything. She remained in this state of mind for about two days and emerged from it slowly to begin to grapple with what was happening to her. For other women the period of mental paralysis lasts longer, sometimes taking them into the second trimester of pregnancy, when abortion procedures are more complicated and costly.

To fully understand the reasons for denial it helps to remember the context in which these experiences take place. Most women swim in a sea of negativity about their sexuality and receive little social support for making choices that step outside of patriarchal definitions of how to be a woman.

Given the confusion and pressure around crisis pregnancy it is all the more impressive that the vast majority of women attend to the situation early in pregnancy, make their decisions and choices, and go on with their lives. Close to ninety percent of all abortions occur within the first trimester of pregnancy.[40]

Sexual Planning

Just as women's spirituality has been idealized, reviled, dismissed, and otherwise shaped according to men's understanding, so, too, has our experience of sexuality.

—SHERRY RUTH ANDERSON AND
PATRICIA HOPKINS, *THE FEMININE FACE OF GOD*

T HERE IS NOTHING WRONG WITH HAVING AN ABORTION. IT is a legitimate, necessary choice. It is one of four possible outcomes of pregnancy: giving birth to a baby and keeping it, giving birth to a baby and giving the infant up for adoption, having a miscarriage, and having an abortion. Abortion is no worse or better an outcome than the other three.

Pregnancy occurs under different circumstances and for different reasons. If we berate ourselves for having become pregnant we are engaging in self-abuse. Being unhappy about it is no reason to beat ourselves up for it. Beating ourselves up doesn't restore the control we feel we have lost.

Sometimes pregnancy occurs as a result of not using birth control. Sometimes it happens even though a method is used. No method of birth control is 100 percent effective. Each has reasons why it fails some of the time.

It is difficult to use birth control. It takes focused energy and time to learn how the methods work and what their medical effects might be. Some methods work better than others. Personal convenience is a factor. So, too, is being able to remember.

Condoms break, diaphragms slip, IUDs dislodge, pills are forgotten.

Some women feel guilty for planning sexual activity. They rationalize this by saying they want sex to be "spontaneous" and "natural." They don't want to have to think about it. They feel embarrassed. They feel good about it and bad about it at the same time.

Media messages reinforce women's confusion. Birth control methods are usually not shown in passionate sexual scenes in movies. We don't hear the man asking the woman if she is using birth control. We don't hear them agree about the use of a condom.

Sex in movies occurs outside of other life considerations. It is not discussed easily or openly. Sex is usually portrayed as a woman and a man overtaken by passion with the man in the dominant position. When are we shown the female lead in a movie going to a clinic or doctor's office for a pregnancy test a few weeks after that fiery love scene? The message is that birth control is a disruptive rather than a natural part of sexual activity.

Unfortunately, family planning clinics and organizations contribute to our confusion by calling birth control services *family* planning. It is an incomplete term. Family planning is only one aspect of the use of birth control methods. Most women and men are not planning families when they use birth control. They are planning sex. They are engaging in *sexual planning*.

Both women and men need to be realistic and honest about their intentions in relationships. We all need to learn to match our behavior with our intentions. We need to carefully examine what we think and feel about being sexual with another person and how this changes over time.

Ideally people would make their decisions about pregnancy before the physical fact of it. A widely shared goal among women is to come to a time when abortion is only an occasional or rare method of birth control. Achieving this will require the cultivation of conscious awareness about sexual matters. This necessarily includes differentiating between sex and reproduction.

Wanting and Not Wanting to Be Pregnant

For some women the urge to be pregnant is strong. They are aware from an early age that they'd like to have children. A general or underlying desire to get pregnant sometimes operates as a barrier to the use of birth control. Sexual activity takes place in an atmosphere of ambivalence. Clarity about wanting to be pregnant is confused by time. We feel conflicted because we know we want to be pregnant at some point in our lives but don't know when. This conflict, coupled with the belief that pregnancy is the only legitimate reason to have sexual intercourse, might make it difficult or impossible to use a method of birth control.

Many feelings and beliefs operate outside of awareness, which magnifies the challenge of using birth control methods consistently. Additionally, if a woman judges her feelings about pregnancy as irrational she will find it more difficult to think through the complexity of her sexual choices.

It is normal to want to be pregnant. It is normal not to want to be pregnant. It is possible for these opposing desires to operate in the same woman at the same time. If she can become aware of her ambivalence, she can begin to prioritize and plan.

The key to coping with oppositional emotions is to honor their existence equally. This can feel scary. A woman may fear that if she were to allow herself to feel the desire to be pregnant she would lose control over her ability to prevent pregnancy. In fact, the opposite is more likely to be true. Strong feelings need to be recognized. If they are not acknowledged consciously they do everything possible to get our attention. This includes influencing us to do things we will regret later, like risking pregnancy. By bringing out the desire for pregnancy a woman is more likely to gain rather than lose control over when it is to occur.

There is room in our inner lives for all our thoughts and feelings. Imagination and fantasy are not subject to the constraints of time and space. They have different parameters because they do not operate in the physical realm. There is satisfaction and relief when we allow ourselves to think and feel all that we think and feel.

Sex and Violence

Childhood sexual abuse and sexual assault cripple a woman's ability to say yes or no to sexual activity. If incest or rape has remained in the underground of her conscious memory, she might find it difficult to take charge of birth control. If, in addition, she believes that sex is bad or that it is mainly to please men, it might be impossible for her to protect herself against pregnancy.

Unfortunately, many women are in relationships where they are subjected to physical violence and emotional coercion and manipulation. If this is the case, it is unlikely that a woman will feel safe to assert herself sexually independent of what her husband or boyfriend wants. Her use or nonuse of birth control methods might occur behind the scenes without any direct communication with him.

A woman who has been sexually abused or assaulted, especially as a child, is likely to fear sex and feel the loss of personal power she associates with it. Unconscious psychic material related to past traumatic experiences might cause her to mentally dissociate from present sexual experiences. As she unconsciously seeks to protect herself from violation in the past, she is unable to protect herself from pregnancy in the present.

A woman who knows she would like to take the necessary measures to prevent pregnancy but finds herself unable to do so, can benefit considerably from discussing her predicament with a counselor who is knowledgeable and sensitive about the issues.

Premeditated Sex

A woman might believe she does not need birth control because she "doesn't do it very much." *It* refers to sexual intercourse. Women who feel discomfort and shame around sexuality find it difficult to say sexual words in conversation. Women who are unable to accept the legitimacy of their sexuality might prefer to play ovarian roulette rather than be guilty of premeditated sex. If a woman believes it is bad to be sexual she might feel even worse to plan it. In this way of thinking, using birth control methods indicates the conscious planning of something bad.

If pregnancy occurs from intercourse in which a woman was unwilling or unable to protect herself she might perceive it as punishment for having done something bad. She might use the pain of an abortion to punish herself for having had sex and become pregnant.

Internalization of antisexual, antiwoman, and antihuman ideas from the dominant patriarchal culture creates a vicious cycle of self-blame. Untangling oneself from this snarled state is an arduous task. But, as women become aware that they no longer want to hurt themselves by engaging in risky behavior, the tightly woven fabric of sexual oppression begins to unravel. The non-use of birth control is one of these behaviors.

Saying Yes, Saying No

To use birth control methods consistently, a woman needs to know whether she wants to have sexual intercourse. She must not assume that she does and she must not assume that she doesn't. She must give herself the benefit of the doubt and allow herself to change her mind.

She might need to ask herself some candid questions like: How much freedom is there in the sexual situations in which I'm likely to be making my choices? Is the man I'm with making all the sexual decisions and taking all the initiative sexually? Is he taking any responsibility for birth control? Is it possible to talk with him about it? Am I willing to risk caring for myself because of the awkwardness of talking about sex? Can I get beyond the feeling of being bad?

When a woman is aware of her situation and the limitations in which she is operating, she is better able to make effective sexual choices. When we pay attention to our needs, our self-esteem grows and we feel stronger about planning the sexual part of our lives. Our outlook on sexual relationships becomes clearer as we learn about our needs and when our needs are met.

Birth Control, Pregnancy, and Other Life Demands

Another condition for the effective use of birth control is to live in an environment that is conducive to taking good care of ourselves and getting our needs met. If a woman is worried about where the money is going to come from for her or her children's next meal, birth control might seem like a distant priority. If she is under stress from her job or unemployed and looking for a job she might not be able to concentrate on making conscious decisions about her sex life.

If she is juggling many responsibilities and children are dependent on her, she might feel she is taking care of all she can handle. If she or someone she loves is in crisis, or she is involved in a natural upheaval such as an earthquake or flood, birth control might be the farthest thing from her mind.

Realistically though, even with serious personal and social problems, it's still a good idea to be committed to the use of birth control. When life is tough, the last thing women need is an unwanted pregnancy.

Abortion is a legitimate method of birth control, but it is an after-the-fact one and the most difficult to tolerate emotionally. If a woman can successfully protect herself from unwanted pregnancy her life will be easier. If that is not possible she might decide to have an abortion.

While knowing whether we want to be pregnant at any given moment can be difficult, tackling the ambivalence about pregnancy helps women to be more aware of other life choices as well. In the United States women have more possibilities for creative activity than ever before. These activities can be in addition to or instead of pregnancy. Dealing with the place of pregnancy in our lives helps to clarify where the other choices fit.

Sexual Relations and Creativity

Unequal emotional power between women and men leads to many unwanted pregnancies. Assumptions about female submission and male dominance blunt the free flow of pleasurable experiences. Fear about stepping outside unspoken rules of right and wrong ways of being sexual can prevent couples from talking about their true needs and desires as individuals.

Sexual energy is not female or male. It is androgynous, human. It can be expressed in myriad ways by anyone, female or male, gay or straight, or mixed gender. It's unfortunate that one of the most physically pleasurable activities for humans is presented by the institutions of society as merely a function of mating for physical reproduction.

When we look beyond the physical we see that while sex is a way to reproduce ourselves, the more common way human beings re-create themselves is psychically—psychologically, mentally, and spiritually. Psychic self-creation, which is ongoing whether or not we are aware of it, requires that we bring conscious awareness to the physical challenges presented by our bodies, namely the prevention of pregnancy and sexually transmitted diseases.

Sexual partners need to talk to each other about sex. It can be more spontaneous and fun when clarity and mutual respect have been created through a consistent commitment to self- enhancing, loving communication between lovers.

In society today, sex is treated in ways that reflect the contradictions of repression. We take it either too seriously or not seriously enough. It is both romanticized and debased. Interest in it is obsessive. It is also ignored. Within marriage it is sanctified. Outside of marriage it is denied, condemned, and commodified. Titillation often takes the place of full, honest sexual expression.

The fact is, sexuality is the same no matter how we organize it socially. The energy of sexuality runs through our bodies regardless of our age, sex, position in society, sexual orientation, family situation, profession, or attitude. Societal labels distort and inhibit the expression of sexuality. Thus, sex is viewed in limited ways and limited to genital activity.

When most people refer to sex they are referring to heterosexual genital intercourse. *Having sex* usually means engaging in sexual intercourse. Kissing and caressing, using the hands and mouth, and giving attention to other parts of the body in addition to the genital area, are usually thought of as *foreplay.* It might be referred to as *being sexual.* However, the idea of having sex usually doesn't include activities that engage the body's senses sexually if no sexual intercourse takes place. Actually though, there are other ways to have sex. For the body, pleasure is pleasure. It makes no difference if the pleasure comes in the form of one act or another.

Pleasuring the body is natural and good. It is a part of being human. It comes naturally for babies and young children. They will sexually stimulate themselves and each other if not interfered with by an adult who has been taught to be fearful about sex. They will assume it is safe to be sexual unless shown otherwise. Children are given minimal guidance about sexual matters, and that guidance is often offered awkwardly. For many kids it is nonexistent.

As we grow up we learn in gentle and harsh ways that sex is an uncomfortable subject not easily discussed, often avoided, and sometimes misused. We hear that sex is an expression of love, but the pleasurable and emotional nature of sexual activity is played down or left out completely. We are shown that sex is a way to exploit and manipulate others to gain power in relationships. We are left to sort these things out on our own for the most part.

Because of repressive attitudes and emphasis on sex as exclusively for reproduction, the union of females and males during sexual intercourse is mentally separated from other aspects of life. It never actually occurs separately though. It always occurs in the context of the rest of our lives and the life of society. Keeping it separate in our minds leads to distortions in intimate relationships and confusion about our needs and desires. It also leads to untimely and sometimes disastrous pregnancies.

Since intercourse is usually considered the goal of being sexual, orgasm—the ecstatic release of energy during sexual activity—is also associated with intercourse. This reinforces the idea that sex is about reproduction. The more this association persists, the more likely a woman is to become pregnant.

Prevention of unwanted pregnancy will occur through changing ways of thinking and behaving. When women feel whole, valid, and in control of their lives they will be able to consistently assert their will about sex and birth control. Healing the pain of experiences with abortion is a way for women to access ourselves sexually and creatively, and thus to bring disparate parts of ourselves together.

Societal changes must occur that create the safety and security people need to behave in ways that serve their individual needs and respect the needs of others. Given the nature of the times in which we live, this is not yet possible on a widespread scale, yet it is the direction in which human evolution is headed.

There is a great deal to discover about sexual relations, and most people will have to educate themselves about the truth of human sexuality. What most people think they know about sex is distorted and missing important pieces. Many of the assumptions are based on centuries of ignorance and misinformation.

As women and men create themselves, so do they create each other. Their relationships exist as extensions of themselves. When we engage our sexual energy in relationship we merge and weave ourselves to create ecstatic experiences for the self. The ecstasy of free sexual expression is an experience of creation. Freed from its exclusive association with reproduction it is revealed as a light, joyful exchange of loving energy.

If sex were treated as the human play that it is, people might be encouraged to express themselves sexually from the time they were children. How would it be if parents and other adults explained how sex works and then let children play and practice to see how they felt about it? What if sexuality were not categorized as heterosexual, homosexual, marital, premarital, or extramarital? Surely life would be more peaceful.

If human relations were respectful and equal, life would be safe and secure for everyone. No one would want to dominate anyone else. No one would ever want to abuse anyone else. Taking responsibility would be no different from loving ourselves. Caring for and about others would be a natural part of self-expression.

In an atmosphere of equality and respect, people would engage the energy of sexuality to bring joy and love into the world. Awareness about preventing or allowing pregnancy would be a vital part of sexual activity. The freedom to make conscious choices would be fully integrated into individual self-concept and behavior. At no time would anyone level negative judgments against themselves or others. Sexuality would be fully joined with all other aspects of life and treated respectfully as a spiritual expression of life.

Tapping into Our Wholeness

Pregnancy can be an opportunity for a woman to contact deeper levels within herself. The brief visit from another presence gives her a chance to get in touch with Spirit. This leads her to an important part of accessing spirituality—the process of gaining respect for self and taking responsibility for herself in relationship to the greater scheme of things. Spirituality often seems otherworldly because we have not come up with a way to put love in the center of societal organization. The reordering of society from inequality and hierarchy to one based on loving relationships will direct us to abolish domination and exploitation in all areas, and raise the life of Spirit to the center of our living world.

Another tension in society is between the innate creativity of individuals and the conditions that deny expression of our creativity. An individual striving for wholeness will naturally seek self-expression through creativity. Historically in patriarchy, women's creativity has often been limited to and by pregnancy. Thus, at this time in history, when women are moving towards greater self-expression, some of us are confronting and decreasing these limitations through our choices in pregnancy.

Life experiences that teach us about death and cycles of renewal take us into the realm of Spirit. As a woman is released to experience herself as a life giver she is faced with her role in death in pregnancy. As she learns more about the death that is part of abortion she comes fully into her life as a woman.

When we look to the natural world we see that death is natural. The killing frost appears every year. Leaves die on the trees so the trees can reappear newly leaved. Nature shows us the wholeness of Life and the cycles of Life. Life gives us what we need to be whole. Wholeness is the manifestation of our creative nature, our connection with Spirit, the higher and deeper consciousness, the All-That-Is.

When a woman taps into her wholeness—her holiness—she connects with a greater consciousness of being. The greater consciousness includes all of life and is guided by love. Love is the essential impulse that activates and motivates all of life. Expression of loving connection to Life is at the core of religious impulses. It is the foundation of spiritual forms, whether they are modest and personal or organized on a grand scale.

Pregnancy expands a woman's knowledge of herself as a female human being. It connects her with the sacredness of Life in female terms. It reminds her that she is part of creation and that her creativity in Life is a natural part of being human.

Women's ability to bring life through the body is a profound expression of Spirit, materializing on a physical level. When we turn it back, when we redirect it, we express our creative, spiritual nature as much as when we bring it through. Having an abortion or a miscarriage is as much an expression of women's spirituality as is giving birth.

Each of the three possible outcomes of pregnancy—birth, miscarriage, and abortion—carries a statement about woman's essential nature as woman. Each expresses the intrinsic power of the female body and consciousness to connect spiritually with primal life forces.

Spiritual Paradoxes

*Reclaiming our reproduction means embracing it, cele-
brating it as the joyous miracle that it is, while at the same
time affirming that it is not the totality of our existence,
that we have needs, visions and potentials as broad and
varied as the rest of humanity.*

—KATHLEEN MCDONELL, *NOT AN EASY CHOICE*

CELIE WAS IN HER EARLY FORTIES AND HAD BEEN RAISED
Catholic. She was the mother of two teenage children, and had
been divorced for about two years. I first saw her in counseling when she
was trying to decide what to do about a pregnancy that had resulted from
the failure of her diaphragm, which she said she used "religiously." She
was in a relationship with a man who made her feel comfortable and supported. They had been seeing each other for less than a year when the
pregnancy occurred.

Celie was intelligent, sensitive, and knowledgeable about herself. She
had cultivated a keen awareness of the complexity of the issues she was
dealing with. She felt sure that she did not want another child. She said she
did not want to "start over with another baby."

Celie felt responsible for her two children and needed to put energy into caring for them as they negotiated their teenage years. She was acutely aware that the three of them were still in the midst of resolving feelings of anger and loss about the divorce. Though she was enjoying her relationship with her current partner, she felt she could not realistically predict whether they would stay together.

Celie considered herself a basically happy person. She felt that her life was going well. She was a teacher of young children and enjoyed her work. She had many personal projects and trips planned that she had been waiting to do for many years. She felt sure that she wanted an abortion because "it's the wrong time." Conflict about the decision had to do with her belief that "it is a life," a belief she related directly to having been raised as a Catholic.

She did a meditation to contact the energy in her uterus and ask for guidance. She was able to do this, and reported that the response she got was that she "could choose to let it stay or not." This surprised her. Next she spent some time in the mountains "connecting with the life force." She said she was becoming aware of how "my body is nonjudgmental," how it "just carries out the body process of pregnancy."

In her next meditation she began a dialogue between her heart center and her pelvic center. She became aware of a sense of "love needing to go out," that perhaps she was "being given a chance to love in a new way." She was also becoming more aware of loss issues with regard to the divorce and her realization that her children were growing up.

Celie was six weeks pregnant when she had the abortion. I saw her again six weeks after the baby would have been born. She was having a difficult time, thinking about the abortion every day and finding herself unable to resolve "the life thing," as she put it.

Though she was "very relieved not to have another child right now," she was holding onto the pregnancy in her mind. Each month, she would find herself both elated and depressed at the possibility of not getting her period. She would cycle through "another mini-pregnancy" in her mind.

Celie was wrestling with the terms to define her experience. Her Catholic upbringing suggested terms of judgment and penance for the "sin" of abortion. She found herself caught up in elaborate fantasies about punishment: fear that something terrible might happen to her children, to her boyfriend, or that she might get cancer.

Different concepts pulled at her as well, concepts that embraced ideas of caring and love and service, concepts that were softer and more fluid.

"I have so much love for these kids!" Celie exclaimed. "Since the abortion, I have so much love for the kids," she said again. "The kids" were the children in her elementary school classroom. She was awed by the love she was feeling. It was an expansive open sense of unlimited generosity. Though she had always enjoyed teaching, what she was feeling now was qualitatively different and she had not felt it before. She wondered if this new feeling was somehow a direct result of the emotional pain she had gone through. Was it the spiritual "purpose" of the abortion?

Celie decided to join an abortion support group to explore her questions. In the group she received validation for her choice of abortion, and understanding about her ambivalence and confusion.

Another woman in the group, Molly, was grappling with some of the same issues as Celie. She too had been raised a Catholic. Molly's conflicts were as much about sexuality as they were about the issue of killing in abortion. Her moral dilemma was expressed vividly in her dreams:

> *I had a whole series of dreams after the abortion with Satan in them....*
> *I was kind of in a state where my eternal soul was in the hands of*
> *Satan. And he was a great guy. I liked him. He was fun to be around.*
> *He was just a nice guy. I remember saying to him, "You're Satan, and*
> *I just really like you." Then I got a flash of pure evilness from him, and*
> *I woke up right at that moment. I was really scared.*

When she began to articulate her feelings about having had an abortion she felt very confused:

There's a lot of emotional stuff, anger and loss, and a lot of that stuff,
and I've been having a real hard time.... I feel like it's just really upset
my value system. If the way I've always thought about good and bad,
right and wrong, doesn't apply, then what is there? In my old way of
thinking, I'm a murderer, and I guess I killed my child. But I don't feel
like I killed my child. I always felt I was a good person, and now I don't
know. I just don't know if I can trust myself anymore.

A little later she said: "There's an incredible anger. It's just there. When
it comes up it's really powerful."

Molly directed a lot of her anger at her boyfriend. She also questioned
the validity of the anger. Celie reassured Molly that her anger was "quite normal." "Because," Celie went on, "it isn't fair, it doesn't seem like it's fair that
you make love with someone, and then you're the one that ends up with the
abortion and the pain. It's just the total unfairness of the whole thing."

For Molly this extended to the sexual situation in which she became
pregnant. Here, too, she was confused:

We'd never slept together before. I told him that I didn't want to sleep
with him. I know it was my fault too. We were making out and the next
thing I knew he was inside me. I said "stop," but it was too late. He
thinks my anger about it is irrational. I blame myself. I don't feel that
it was forced intercourse, but I didn't give him permission either.

Molly worked hard to learn more about herself. The key to her process
was her anger. Though she was afraid of it, she learned to recognize its importance. As she became more comfortable she saw that her anger could
help her to gain clarity about how to understand what had happened to her.

Everything made her mad: the disrespectful way she was treated by her
boyfriend, her passivity about sex, and her religious upbringing, which produced a pervasive guilt about being alive, about being female, and about
being sexual. Until the time of her abortion, Molly had seen herself as a
"good person,"—unselfish and kind, and sexually virtuous. Her awareness

of her sexuality had been only a shadow in the background of her consciousness. Her boundaries in relationships were weak, and she was easily manipulated by others and quick to doubt her own perceptions. Molly's concepts of good and bad were jumbled and confused, creating a crisis in her personal value system.

Her assumptions about what she believed came into question as she searched to find answers to troubling questions and accusations. Was she a bad person? Perhaps a murderer? Was it her fault that she became pregnant?

Her upbringing would affirm that she was to blame for everything that had taken place, but something inside her rose up in rebellion. A voice inside her told her to question her assumptions and beliefs. The rage that came with it pushed her to examine all her patterns in relationships, the dynamics within her family, and her personal and professional goals.

The "good person" she had believed herself to be turned out to be a thin shell, a false self. As she explored her issues she began to see that her rage was about being denied her integrity as a whole person, and about how she participated in that denial. She learned to trust her own perceptions and act in her own interest. Eventually this led to a heightened awareness of choice-making in every area of her life.

As for "the life thing," Celie felt comforted by the knowledge that other women were experiencing similar conflicts in their own ways. The more she shared her feelings and thoughts about the relationship of pregnancy to other aspects of her life, the more she was able to reduce the amount of guilt she carried around with her.

For both Celie and Molly, resolution of distressing emotional and spiritual conflicts required a deep and thorough examination of beliefs and assumptions they didn't know they had, and a willingness to fully grieve the losses in their lives.

Sexuality and Spirituality

One of the most destructive aspects of patriarchal religious dogma is the practice of separating sexuality and spirituality—demonizing sexuality and elevating spirituality above the body. Defining sexuality as bad because it is of the body and because it is human is an effective way of controlling people's behavior. Controlling behavior is one of the main functions of religion when it is practiced in a society structured around dominance and submission.

Sexuality is one of our chief lifelines to ourselves. It is one of the main ways people connect to their spirituality and to their souls. Placing women's bodily experiences outside of and in opposition to spirituality is the main way of enforcing a less than spiritual status for women. The separation maintains the power of patriarchy, the power of masculine over feminine, and the power of men over women.

This benefits neither women nor men. It diminishes humanness because it locks people into artificial categories of sexual identity. The "unfairness of the whole thing" is not about the real physical differences between women and men. It is not about the fact that pregnancy takes place in the female body and psyche. There is nothing unfair about that. The unfairness is the lack of respect for the power of female people to channel pregnancy.

Pregnancy is the grounding of the continuation of all that we can be. It brings the nonphysical into the physical. It is a high experience of sexuality. It is an expression of women's sexual nature. It connects us to ourselves. It connects us to Spirit. Pregnancy is a primal expression of Earth's continuous regeneration. It is the physical ground of Earth manifesting through our bodies. Sexuality is the electricity that unites us with Nature. It is sacred and inviolable.

Women's sexual self-expression is reflected in our choices in relationships. This includes decisions regarding whom we connect with and when we do the connecting. Our choices in self-expression depend on our ability to be in touch with our feelings and needs and to know that these might change. It requires that we give ourselves access to all options, breathing space in which to feel different possibilities, and the benefit of the doubt that we know what is best for ourselves.

The spirituality of sexuality and pregnancy has been recognized down through the millennia in the tradition of the Great Goddess and religions that recognize the sacredness of the natural world. These traditions recognize the feminine principles of creation, life cycles, and transformation as central to spiritual connection and life. The life giving power of women is considered central to the life of the human community.

The appearance of abortion in the center of social controversy at this time in history is a coming together of myriad issues that are having an impact on human life at this time. It brings into focus the imbalances in society due to the inequality of the sexes. An individual woman caught up in the storm of a pregnancy might find her awareness expanding by leaps and bounds as she grasps the depth and richness of what is happening to her.

The spiritual paradoxes we encounter when dealing with abortion will be influenced by our spiritual worldview and our way of approaching spirituality in our lives. As we explore the issues we will find that they link to many other issues in our lives, especially sexuality and relationships. We might find ourselves making mental connections between events in our lives that we did not think were connected.

Themes of connection and separation come up over and over again when dealing with abortion. The interplay of connection and separation is at the core of spiritual development. Unity of self with self, and self with other, is at the center of the experience of pregnancy. Profound joy and sorrow define the emotional parameters of these primal polarities.

Pregnancy embodies the spiritual dichotomy of separation and connection. The relationship of a woman to a fetus is totally connected and at the same time separate—two beings bound as one. Because it isolates women from societal approval, abortion might bring us into contact with parts of our existence that feel separate but in fact are connected to All Life. The shock waves of the experience sometimes demand that we recognize our spirituality in new ways.

Reluctance to explore the spiritual dimension of abortion usually originates from fear of judgment and punishment. Of course, this varies among individuals from different religious backgrounds, but there is little doubt that patriarchal religious dogma is one of the main causes of psychological distress for women facing crisis pregnancy and abortion.

Major religious organizations tend to reinforce the concept of God as judgmental, punitive, authoritarian male energy. This picture of God restricts a woman from moving beyond a limited, oppressive concept of her experience and her feelings about herself. If a woman must be forgiven for her sins by a judging god, she is automatically labeled a sinner. Even more, it strips her of her inner authority to forgive herself and usurps her ability to be a moral being in her own right. It compromises her integrity as a capable individual who can take moral responsibility for making decisions about sexual issues.

A woman who finds herself in a spiritual crisis as a result of an abortion might find the self-hatred and self-blame she feels intolerable. She might have to reconsider the idea of giving authority to God as a punitive male figure. As she faces her inner conflicts she might find that none of her usual ways of thinking apply to her experience with abortion. The process of self-examination is likely to lead to an encounter with an ancient and long forgotten spiritual and moral authority that she carries within herself.

A crisis pregnancy presents women with an opportunity (often also unwanted!) to define our personal belief systems. We can clarify our thoughts about the meaning and value of life in general and our own lives. Regardless of the outcome of a pregnancy, the experience provides a chance for us to deepen our knowledge of ourselves. In addition, we can more fully examine our beliefs about the realm of what we call *God.*

Soul Life

I have a strong sense of the continuity and connected nature of soul life, but exactly how it works is not clear to me. I am fascinated by the idea that we *call in* our experiences to resolve karmic issues. This is part of a way of thinking that sees life as the flow and interaction of forms of energy, both physical and nonphysical. It gives credence to reincarnation and the idea that the soul enters physical life with intention. I don't know if it's true, but it rings true and seems possible if we look at life as an elaborate design of lessons.

Intuitives with whom I have spoken about abortion tell me that "the woman calls the fetus in" to resolve some sort of issue in her life. That grabs my attention, but is it really what happens? Do we call things in or do things happen and we have a deep capacity to wrap our consciousness around them and weave them into our understanding? Either way, we are called upon to rise to the occasion of understanding our experience.

The creative process of our lives—the way we create ourselves—includes anything and anyone who comes our way. Our challenge is to learn how to be in right relationship with all the different aspects of our lives and to become aware of the spiritual essence of Life. (It is not necessary to believe in karma or reincarnation to do this.)

Sometimes we set intentions for ourselves without even realizing it. We say we want our lives to go in a particular direction. Then we forget that we put this intention out and go about our business. Later, something happens (often when we least expect it) that brings us the raw material for building a better understanding of how we are living. In that sense, we call in experiences. It's just that they often don't look like anything we would have wanted because we didn't realize what we were asking for.

If we expand this discussion into the historical sphere, it takes on a different dimension. Perhaps history is calling in pregnancies that will show women how to be powerful and whole. The life of soul and spirit happens in the context of the evolution of the Earth. It is human nature to create social networks—tribes, clans, and societies. Patriarchy, along with its economic systems, has been dominant within these for over five thousand years. The evolution of the Earth and Nature, which includes humans, is evolving out of patriarchy into ways of living that honor the equality of life forms. A cultural form such as legal abortion provides a vehicle that can help us pick up some of the missing pieces of our understanding.

We can apply this understanding in our personal lives by remembering to spend time in the natural, more-than-human world, with animals and plants that live alongside us. We can meditate on and with the land that supports our lives, regardless of whether this is land covered by concrete in a city, a yard behind our house, a park, or a wilderness area. We can consult with the greater body of the Earth, as our own body-mind-soul-spirit wraps itself around a problem pregnancy.

It is more than the soul life of an individual woman or fetus that is at stake here. It is the Soul of the Earth as well. We are being asked to turn our attention to developing a broader, deeper consciousness about Life, a consciousness that includes both the responsibility for the emergence of new life and the recognition of the importance of playing an intentional and positive role in that process.

If we are to survive as a species, human beings are going to have to accept that our bodies and the body of the Earth are one and the same. We must engage consciously with the life cycles—the coming into being and going away of life through death—and respect those individuals who are put in the position of making direct decisions about that in specific situations.

Lisa

Lisa, a thirty-three-year-old woman, confided to me that through conscious negotiation between her soul and another soul she had been able to mentally induce a spontaneous abortion. The way she described it, her miscarriage occurred twenty-four hours after an intense energy merge with the visiting soul, which created sufficient vibration in her body to cause a change in the physical status of the pregnancy, bringing on uterine contractions and the expulsion of the fetus from her body. She said the visiting soul then departed.

She was sixteen years old at the time, and aware that she had highly developed intuitive abilities and sensitivities. Along with this knowledge about herself, she was aware of her emotional immaturity. She asked the visiting soul for help. She spoke directly to it in meditation. She explained that if it were to come all the way through a full term pregnancy, it would probably be neglected or abused because she was not ready or willing to provide for its care.

Lisa created a conscious soul-to-soul agreement about the direction of her pregnancy. This is not always possible, nor is it what happens for all women, but more likely than not, it is more common than is generally known. The dynamics of spiritual negotiation are dependent upon the nature of a woman's awareness, her level of spiritual development, and whether she has access to the tools for inner exploration. Most women are unaware that anything is going on in the realm of soul. Whatever the specifics of the situation, there are always lessons to be learned.

Nonphysical Life

Much of life is a process of energy exchange, movement of energy from one form to another. Pregnancy is an opportunity to participate in a process of development on a number of levels. Seeing it as an energy exchange provides a better understanding of the relationship between physical and nonphysical life.

Soul is the place of essence of a human being. It is a unity of vital energies and the place of our deepest longings. It is timeless and moves through human life as a way of connecting us to each other and to the Universe. Its primary qualities are: learning, teaching, and connecting about issues of existence. It functions without judgment to bring understanding and knowledge about life and relationships and to connect us to a Unity of Being that is the All of Life.

Operating out of a perspective that includes the existence of soul defies many of the usual ways of thinking about time and space. It offers the opportunity to embrace spiritual realities. When we acknowledge that soul energy is guiding and connecting, we are able to relax into life and follow the lessons as they unfold.

It is likely that the individual energy of spiritual essence—soul—that is attracted to connecting to the fetus in pregnancy is in an intermediate stage of relationship to the physical plane. This means that the entering soul is engaged in a process of spiritual negotiation with the woman in whose body the pregnancy is located.

The negotiation process could be conscious for the woman, but in most cases, it is unconscious. Self-doubt produced by fear, combines with beliefs that tell us it is not possible to be aware of things like this. As a result, we are prevented from becoming cognizant of the process. High levels of fear coupled with low levels of social support can make it impossible to engage consciously with the soul level of the decision making process. When clarity remains elusive, decisions can be made that go against the self. Actions are taken that are riddled with confusion and misunderstanding. Sometimes, mistakes are made. (This is all the more reason to make *all* options in pregnancy safe, legal, and readily available.) Some women are aware of the onset of pregnancy at the moment of conception. Others speak of a presence before, during, and sometimes after pregnancy with which they are able to communicate through their thoughts. Others are not aware of a presence at all.

The more aware a woman is, psychically as well as physically, the more she will be able to participate in the power of the pregnancy process. As she negotiates her life and the life of a potential other person she gains knowledge about what is important in life and how to make choices. If this awareness is gained after an abortion it is no less important. As we move through the abortion experience we are given the opportunity to learn how to respect and love ourselves and our place in Life.

When a woman does not want to bring through another soul in pregnancy, it is up to her to communicate that desire. Our intentions are of utmost importance. If we approach our decisions in a direct and loving manner without fear or guilt, we will find less agony in the process of the separation of souls. Prior to having an abortion, one woman confided that while sitting in meditation, she "saw the spirit of the baby leave." She said it looked "like a little blue light taking off into space." Shortly after, she completed the process on a physical level by undergoing a surgical abortion procedure.

It might be that the energy of spiritual essence organized in the soul does not place the value of the physical *over* the value of the nonphysical. It might not be the intention of a visiting soul to come all the way into the physical plane. Pregnancy is part of the process of bringing the nonphysical into the physical. A developing embryo or fetus is an energy mass in physical form with its own distinct characteristics. It is joined with the energy of the woman in whom it is developing. Because it is part of her body, it is entirely dependent upon her for its physical existence and development. However, its spiritual existence is related to the energies of spirit outside itself and in between the physical and nonphysical. The choice to stay or leave will depend upon the contract forming within the woman. In the matter of energetic and organic negotiation the pregnant woman is at once a party in the negotiation and a container for the process.

What is important in the negotiation process is clarity of intention and honest communication. Conscious decision making about life in pregnancy is a serious matter, not one to be taken lightly. Soul relations are of the deepest kind. Negotiating soul to soul is a delicate matter and must be approached gently and with full integrity.

So, what happens to a visiting soul that tries to connect during pregnancy? Most likely, given the expansive nature of Spirit, when a woman chooses to discontinue a pregnancy and have an abortion, the soul around the pregnancy leaves. Would it return to another pregnancy at another time? Possibly, possibly not.

In *Soul Contracts*, Linda Baker, a registered nurse and spiritual healer, describes "spiritual abortion" sessions she facilitates for women. She guides them into deep trance states, which provide the opportunity to communicate with "the child's spirit" about the desire not to continue the pregnancy. She has documented cases of successful spontaneous abortions and deep emotional healing.[41]

The soul energies we contact around some pregnancies might be coming in to help women learn how to make choices. With regard to the continuum between nonphysical and physical life, they can probably go either way. Does this sound like a self-serving rationalization to assuage guilty feelings? Perhaps, but I think not. If anything, thinking about the spiritual life of pregnancy allows women to face difficult feelings like fear and guilt while embracing gentler possibilities. As we learn to care for and respect ourselves, we become capable of bringing life through our bodies that has a promise of being loved and cared for in the physical world.

Having an abortion is an opportunity to turn towards ourselves and examine the ways in which we conduct ourselves in our lives. We might find that we want to let go of ways of living in the world that don't nurture us. Letting go of a pregnancy can be an opportunity to let go of aspects of our lives that are no longer serving us. We can allow new ways of seeing and being to enter our awareness by actively engaging in the process of letting go.

Internal resistance to the process of letting go might indicate fear of the emotionality of the grief that usually comes with it. Facing that fear allows the process of growth to move along and fulfill its intended mission. Most likely, we will find that our grief, though confusing and painful, is tolerable and helpful in taking us where we need to go. Resolution of spiritual conflicts comes naturally when losses are fully grieved.

Grief

*Tom and I are finally recovering from all the unexpected
emotional roller coaster rides. I think being over all the
physical symptoms has allowed me to put it aside a little
more. I had lots of dreams of drowning children for a
while. I'm smart enough to recognize that meant I wasn't
dealing with something. One night I sat down and cried,
mourned in a way, and Tom held me. Today, running at
sunrise, I noticed: the morning sky reflected in gutter
water holds summer clouds completely.*

—A WOMAN, TWO WEEKS AFTER AN ABORTION

ACULTURE THAT DENIES THE VALIDITY OF A WOMAN'S PRO-
creative power robs her of her grief as well. It does not follow
that a woman who feels grief about an abortion is a murderer, nor does
it imply that she should not have had an abortion. Grief about an abortion, like any other kind of grief, is about loss. It is a natural process of
human nature. The fact that it was a consciously induced loss does not
alter the basic dynamics of loss and grief.

Abortion is pregnancy loss. If a woman feels loss, it is natural to grieve.
If she feels only relief, it's unlikely that she will need to grieve the loss. It is

not unusual to feel a mixture of sadness and relief. It is not possible to predict exactly how we will feel about the loss of a pregnancy.

Consciously controlling the process of pregnancy and deciding to turn back a pregnancy often produces a mix of feelings, which includes sadness and loss. Even if a woman feels relieved and happy about having an abortion, she might need to grieve the loss of the pregnancy and everything it represented in her life.

The arrival of the menstrual period during the first few months after an abortion reminds a woman that she is no longer pregnant. For some women this is cause for celebration. For others it precipitates a drop into sadness, and is a painful reminder of the loss of the pregnancy. Some women experience a mix of feelings, a bittersweet blend of gratitude and lost possibilities.

Having an abortion is a process of letting go of present possibilities to allow new possibilities to develop. The time between, when the pregnancy is gone and the new has not yet appeared, feels like a void. The relief felt by most women appeases the emptiness somewhat. Balance is restored when the void is filled with the energy of new creation. This can happen immediately or it can take years. If the feeling of emptiness goes on for a long time, a woman might become at risk for depression.

The energy of new creation can take many forms. It might take the form of an ongoing project. It might be a creative effort that we've been wanting but have never gotten around to doing. It might be a time of upheaval and major life transition. It might be a time of self-contemplation and reexamination of one's life direction and priorities. It might be another pregnancy.

The loss of connection with a pregnancy creates a need for loving connection with others. The time right after an abortion is a vulnerable time for most women, and the need for loving attention and nurturing is high. Many women feel uncomfortable needing and asking for support, so they try to manage on their own, get through it as quickly as possible, and go on with their lives. By not paying attention to their feelings and needs they hope to make them go away.

The belief that no one will be there for her and that she has to take care of everything on her own, might lead a woman to put up emotional walls—walls around her heart. By doing so, she maintains the strength to manage her fears while making arrangements for an abortion and continuing to function in her life.

If she has experiences in her life that have shown her she cannot count on others to help her, she will not be likely to involve anyone in her pain no matter how close they are to her. She may want more than anything just to be held by her boyfriend, but she might not be able to say a word about it to him.

A woman may be surprised that her boyfriend or husband has his own feelings of sadness. Two people can give each other comfort when they grieve together. It is a loving thing for a woman and a man to express their feelings to and with one another. It builds trust and a sense that *I'm not in this alone.*

Grieving losses is not part of daily life for most people. Most people have learned not to "dwell" on unpleasant or difficult experiences. We try to put painful times behind us as fast as possible. This does not usually work very well in the life of the emotions. If an experience needs to be grieved it will produce symptoms to get a person's attention. These might include:

- A sense of contraction in the body
- Shallow breathing
- Feelings of isolation and separateness
- Low energy
- Fatigue
- Feelings of disorientation
- Difficulty concentrating
- Spontaneous crying
- Emotional numbness
- Heightened sensitivity to one's surroundings
- Disrupted sleep patterns

- Anxiety about being alone
- Low tolerance of stress
- Thoughts about death
- Feelings of sadness
- Feelings of anger, fear, irritability, or anxiety
- Feelings of guilt and helplessness

Permission to Grieve

Patricia was thirty-four and the mother of three grade school children. Since her abortion two months before, Patricia was having difficulty sleeping and was hardly eating. She felt disoriented and unable to concentrate. She worried that she was developing an eating disorder. Her symptoms were actually more indicative of grief.

At first Patricia seemed defensive about the idea that she might be grieving. She felt guilty and ashamed about her pregnancy and abortion. She questioned her love for her children because she had "killed this one." Since she had willfully ended the pregnancy she felt she had no right to grieve. Her fearfulness about having feelings of sadness and loss had compromised her ability to nourish herself with food.

With permission to feel grief, she was able to open to her sadness about letting go of the pregnancy. She was able to release much of her fear. Her sleeping and eating improved. She spent focused time contemplating the place of the pregnancy in her life, and the meaning for her and her children of her choice to end it.

Patricia was able to incorporate her emotional process into a spiritual practice that had been part of her daily life for many years. This supported and comforted her. As she did not regret her abortion decision, she was able to resolve her guilt relatively quickly. The most acute symptoms of her grief disappeared, though she continued to carry a sense of sadness.

Every year after that, Patricia celebrated the birth and death in her own way. She continued to be aware of her sadness about the loss of the pregnancy, and believed it was important to honor what had happened and what was continuing to happen. She referred to the time of the abortion as "the birthday."

Three years after her abortion Patricia had an experience that changed everything. In her words:

> *It was the spring, close to the birthday. I was lying in my bed. I had a sense that someone was in the room with me. It felt like a presence. A warmth filled the room. It was the spirit of the child! I couldn't believe it! The spirit came back to me and told me that it was okay to have had the abortion, that I had made the right decision and that it was okay. I had been carrying such a heavy sadness and so much warmth came in. I cried. I felt released from that sadness. I felt so much lighter. After that I felt so much better about the abortion and about myself.*

Spiritual experiences are closely related to emotional life. They are felt in the heart. It is not unusual for grief states to set the stage for awareness in the spiritual dimension. Grief can open a person to the reality of the nonphysical through the strong feelings it engenders and the persistence with which it continues until the feelings shift.

Pregnancy can bring a woman to an awareness of the roots of her human connection. Letting go might be wrenching and heartbreaking. There are many reasons why she might not work it through ahead of time. After letting go of a pregnancy, she may be surprised by the pain of this initiation into female reproductive reality.

Pregnancy can bring a woman to the roots of her essential spirituality. The joining of the physical and the spiritual in pregnancy gives us an expanded sense of the flow of life forces. It shows us that Life is spiritual.

As women embody the life process, we are in a continuous relationship with our essential nature. As we learn that our nature, our human nature, is fundamentally relational, we can learn to trust ourselves and our sense of caring in relationships.

Loss of a Chance to Care

Part of the pain of abortion for women and men is an acute sense of the lack of caring in our lives. The longing for caring relationship might produce a deep sadness. The grief experienced is about the loss of a chance to care and to be cared for. It is the loss of a potential relationship with a child and the feeling of being strongly connected to that child.

A woman's relationship with her boyfriend or husband might seem diminished by an abortion. Sometimes it's difficult to pinpoint exactly what has been lost, but there is often a sense that something has been. For some it is the loss of the unity created by the physical pregnancy in the minds of the woman and man involved. For others it is the loss of a dream, the chance to create an ideal life with a baby at the center of it.

A woman may feel angry towards her boyfriend or husband because she believes he doesn't care enough. This kind of anger can be a cover-up for the sadness about the loss of the pregnancy.

A woman might also have a belief operating underneath that had she continued the pregnancy she would have received more caring from others. She may not have been aware until the abortion that she was missing being cared for in her life. It's a good idea to sort these feelings out, to know which of them have direct relevance to the abortion experience and which do not.

Grief about abortion might expose issues of caring in a relationship between a woman and a man. Close examination of each person's feelings and needs can reveal areas in the relationship that need to be attended to. A pregnancy crisis can be a catalyst for two people to begin relating more openly about their feelings.

For some women having an abortion might be the beginning of a process of clarification, of asking themselves, "What *do* I care about? What *is* important to me?" Grieving an abortion might put a woman in touch with her need for community and to be less isolated and more connected to others.

Loss of a Dream

Loss of a pregnancy in abortion is sometimes about the loss of a dream. A woman may be carrying images about how she wants her life to be, about being comfortable in a relationship, having a nice place to live, being secure, relaxed, and happy. Having a baby could represent all of that.

Choosing not to have a baby may confront her with the gap between her fantasies and the life she is living. If she doesn't like what she sees in her life she might be pulled to stay in her fantasies. An abortion might make that impossible. She could feel anger as well as sadness, as she is pushed to let go of her fantasies. If she has been using her fantasies to avoid facing difficulties in her relationship or in other parts of her life, her abortion could be an emotional crash landing.

It is important to grieve the loss of our fantasies—the "what ifs" and the "if onlys."

If two people in relationship share dreams and fantasies, the loss of the dream might put the relationship on shaky ground. If each partner has seen the future potential of the other partner and the relationship, but is not fully participating in the present, the loss of a pregnancy through abortion might be a rude awakening. It may also be a wakeup call and a chance to turn their attention to the relationship as it is and put some energy into it.

Loss of Self

Grief about the loss of a pregnancy, whether through an abortion or a miscarriage, often appears to be entirely about the loss of the child. A woman may find herself thinking about it every day and feeling sad. She might describe her thinking as obsessive because "I can't get the child out of my mind."

While there is no doubt that the feeling of having lost a child might be real, there is another way to understand these feelings. The obsessive quality of the feelings can be a sign that the deeper self is trying to revive the memory of other, older losses, especially the loss of self that often occurs early in life.

All people are born whole, carrying all their potentialities, much like an acorn.[42] Even before we are aware of ourselves we look for ways to express ourselves, to show who we are in the world. As our awareness grows through childhood and adulthood we gain knowledge about ourselves. Our innate gifts and talents become conscious dreams and desires. But most of us are denied expression of our original selves, and thus experience a loss of soul, a going away of parts of the essential self.

This occurs because societal structures are set up to channel people into narrowly defined economic and social roles. Families generally do not nurture their children to be free, but rather to fit into prescribed ways of living. The dominant values are the values of the marketplace. There are "winners" and "losers." People learn to survive rather than to create, to be less rather than more.[43]

This is especially true for women. A male-centered society that values property more than people defines women and everything feminine in negative terms. A little girl receives these negative messages in many ways and in a steady stream. In the last thirty or so years of active feminism, only a small dent has been made in this ancient cultural wall of experience.

Thoughts and images of a child in a pregnancy might stimulate images of oneself as a child. A woman may actually be focusing on her own childhood experience when she focuses incessantly on a little girl or little boy from a pregnancy that might have been. She may be unconsciously trying to contact the child within herself and the times in her life when she experienced the loss of herself. The inner child is an archetypal thought form that represents an essential innocence, a psychic place of pure being, of vulnerability, of joy, wonder, and play. If we have experienced trauma as a child, our inner child might be wounded and frightened.

Loss of Safety

A woman who becomes pregnant when she doesn't want to be will experience her pregnancy as invasive to some degree. As her personal boundaries feel violated, she experiences a loss of security and safety. If she has an abortion she places herself in a vulnerable position physically and emotionally. The degree to which she feels less safe will be influenced by how safe she felt prior to becoming pregnant.

If a woman was using a method of birth control she may feel let down by the method. She might feel angry with her body for "betraying" her. The loss of safety about being sexually active might influence her to back off from sexual intercourse after an abortion. She might have been using a particular method of birth control for some time. She could feel that her preferred method of birth control can't be trusted anymore.

A woman who has led a sheltered, privileged life might be shocked by an unwanted pregnancy more than a woman who has had other insecurities in her life. She might resist letting go of her belief that the world is a safe place. On the other end of the spectrum, another woman might take it for granted that the world is unsafe and that she has little say over events in her life.

When a loss of safety and security occurs due to unintended pregnancy, it is natural to grieve. By paying attention to her feelings a woman can comfort herself and heal from her losses. By acknowledging her loss of security she can become secure again in new ways.

The Energy of Change

Grief contains the emotional energy of change. It is the process through which we recognize and let go of aspects of our lives that are no longer part of our present time environment. The movement of energy in the grief process allows changes to take place in relationships, which put a person in synchrony with the unfolding of her life and her awareness about her life.

Grief is the way we feel changes that are taking place in our lives. Feelings in the grief process include sadness, anger, and relief. A common misconception is that fear is part of grief, but this is not accurate. Fear about grief comes from confusion about grief, the belief that death and loss are bad, and the belief that it is dangerous or wrong to allow ourselves to feel vulnerable emotionally.

When we allow ourselves to grieve freely there is no fear. There is a sense of flowing movement, much like it might feel to be a moving body of water, which, in a way, we are. While the movement of the feelings might seem potentially overwhelming, it is only when they are denied or get stuck that they cause problems.

The key to successful grieving is to create enough space in our lives for the feelings to move through. In addition to whatever we can create personally, this could include "grief leave" on the job (more than a couple of days) and recognition by society that the activity of grieving about our losses is normal, natural, and important. If each emotion in the grief process is greeted with understanding about its value in connecting us to everything with which we are in relationship, we can move more easily through the grief as it moves through us.

If we deny our grief, we are also denying the importance of relationships. If we deny the significance and meaning of events, people, or things, we blunt our experience and cut ourselves off from the fullness of life. When we recognize and acknowledge our losses we honor our relationships and connections to people, things, and events in our lives that have significance and meaning.

Grief is not an occasional process. It is an ongoing part of conscious existence. As we learn to let go of passing parts of our lives, we also gain clarity and strength to go on with our lives. Losses of relationship are inevitable. When we no longer fear our losses we can be free to be fully connected in the present. Grief, when allowed its place in our lives, gives us our relationships.

Anticipatory Grief

If a woman is open to it she can work through feelings of grief and loss before an abortion takes place. One woman I talked with was able to do this by opening to her sadness in several counseling sessions before her abortion procedure.

One night she dreamed that her four-year-old daughter was pulling a small painted wagon towards a graveyard as she followed close behind. After that she made a point of spending more focused time with her daughter because the child's energy was comforting and strengthening to her as she struggled to let go of her attachment to the current pregnancy. By the time she had the abortion procedure, the pain of her grief had almost completely subsided.

Another woman, Joanna, took a week off from work before her abortion "to just be with this," to focus on her feelings about being pregnant and to prepare for an abortion. Her process included feeling some sadness about the loss of her pregnancy, about not having the baby, and about letting go of that direction in her life.

Joanna did not want to have children. When she became pregnant a second time ten years later, she repeated the process of taking time off prior to the abortion. She was able to resolve her grief because she gave herself space in which to do so, and did not have any emotional difficulties after her abortion.

Because an abortion is a consciously planned event, a woman who is aware of feeling attached to her pregnancy may also be aware of grieving about her decision to end the pregnancy. If a significant part of her wants to have the baby, but she has decided it would be best not to, her grief will be present and real.

A woman who experiences strong feelings of grief before an abortion might worry that she is going to continue feeling that way after her abortion. While it is possible that she will, many women find that if they work through their grief before an abortion they are free of painful feelings afterwards. It is not possible to predict how long feelings will last or if and when they might reappear.

Anticipatory grief is feeling a loss emotionally before the loss takes place physically. The idea of the loss triggers feelings about it. Because of the nature of conscious awareness, anticipatory grief is often spontaneous. Feelings take over without any conscious decision. They are just there. A woman can help the feelings move through her by recognizing and honoring them.

The Importance of Ritual

As a woman learns to recognize and validate her grief she may find herself drawn to forms that ritualize her experience. This is a natural tendency when someone drops into the soul level of experience. The soul level—the spiritual dimension—is distinguished by a sense of the movement of an intuitive flow. There is a feeling of being guided by an inner knowingness. It is a centering into a deep level of connectedness with self and the Universe as a whole.

Sometimes when I suggest to a woman that she consider creating a ritual to help resolve her experience with abortion, she asks, "But what should I do?" Often the question reflects her discomfort with the idea of ritual, possibly due to her association of ritual with prescribed religious practices rather than personal spiritual expression. Sometimes it is due to the assumption that a ritual or ceremony has to be elaborate and complicated.

The purpose of ritual is to honor one's experience. What is done is not nearly as important as that something be done. A ritual marks the passage of a life event and forms a unity of meaning about significant aspects of people's lives. Rituals provide forms in which a person can experience her aloneness *and* feel her connection with others, in peace, and without interruption from the demands of daily life.

A ritual creates a unity in time. It acts as a bridge between what has been, what is now, and what is coming. It gives our experiences and feelings a place to call their own. We can be more at ease with the altered states of consciousness caused by intense grief when our thoughts and emotions are channeled into a ritualized form.

I talked with a woman named Nancy about her shame and guilt about two abortions she'd had six and eight years previously. She had been experiencing anxiety, sleep disturbances, and eating binges. She was afraid that if she allowed herself to grieve and to fully feel her feelings, she would "go crazy."

During a meditation to music she relaxed. With her eyes closed, her breathing slowed, and she went inside herself and saw an image of a hillside and of herself "planting something to honor life," to acknowledge "the two babies."

When she returned a week later she told me that she had gone to a hillside in the mountains and created a ritual. In the ritual she named the two babies, wrote letters to them, read the letters out loud to them, buried the letters, and allowed herself to "fall apart." She said she "cried until I couldn't cry anymore." After that she continued to cry on and off for a few days.

I suggested that she set aside some time every day, light a candle, and sit with her feelings and thoughts until the grieving process had taken its course.

Layered Grief

If life losses are not grieved at the time they occur, or soon thereafter, they might pile up and wait to be grieved. The loss of a pregnancy in abortion can expose grief about previous losses. As a woman feels the grief in abortion she discovers the layers of grief underneath. Each loss is an opportunity to grieve all other losses. Remarkable healing might occur both personally and in relationships.

Life is a process of continuous coming into being and going away. Conscious awareness of the process is a sense of loving and letting go. Emotionally, human beings are continuously attaching and disengaging from one another and from all aspects of our experience.

Often disengagement will occur before completion and resolution of the attachment. The grief that results might be denied or ignored. If this is the case a person will be left with a sense of frustrated incompleteness, which feels like emptiness and sadness. Irritability often shows up as well, due to the frustration of not knowing or expressing feelings that are under the surface of awareness. The sadness is often about lost possibilities and unmet needs, and can be debilitating, especially if a person feels isolated from sources of love and emotional support.

By the time a woman is old enough to experience the losses in abortion, she has usually incurred numerous other losses in her life. These might include losses in relationship, family, place, community, life direction, opportunity, health, body, and loss of confidence and security.

Losses that occur early in life are frequently accompanied by loss of self. This is because the losses are often traumatic and there are no socially acceptable ways to follow the experiences through by acknowledging feelings associated with them. The resulting tension and psychic pressure cause parts of the soul-self to leave one's awareness.

The loss of pregnancy in abortion is, for some women, the storm that sends the river of grief over its flood banks. The grief a woman feels about the loss of the pregnancy might also be grief about the death of a parent many years before. It could be about her parents' divorce, or the loss of a favorite pet as a child, or losing the chance to go to college because her family could not afford to send her.

She might need to grieve about the loss of previous pregnancies. She might suddenly become aware that she has suffered a loss of intimacy with her partner. She might find herself feeling profound grief about abuse suffered as a child and the accompanying loss of nurturing.

Once grief is opened it can seem endless. It isn't. It simply asks to be attended to by being acknowledged and felt. It wants to be expressed. Spending time with other people helps, as does writing, reading, drawing, singing, listening to music, playing music, dancing, taking walks, eating good food, creating rituals, sitting quietly, talking with a counselor, and spending time in nature.

If a person tries to escape from her grief, the grief will find another way to show up. If she tries to "get on with life" too soon, without paying attention to her feelings, she will most likely find herself reacting inappropriately to other situations. If she tries to "put it behind her" prematurely she might find that her feelings about small disappointments in her daily life are blown out of proportion because feelings about bigger losses have been pushed away.

Moving Beyond Grief

Grief about abortion is different for different women. It might or might not take up significant emotional time or energy. It might or might not involve other losses. It might be simple or it might be complicated. If a woman's life circumstances provide her with sufficient emotional support she might find she can weather the grief storm relatively easily. If she is grieving many other losses, she might have difficulty moving through the process. Each person's situation and needs are her own.

Spiritual Choices

To pray, you open your whole self to sky, to earth, to sun,
to moon...

—JOY HARJO, "EAGLE POEM"

ALL THINGS IN LIFE ARE INTERCONNECTED. AS OUR AWARE
ness deepens and our hearts open, we gain in our capacity to understand the meaning and place of our experiences in the unfolding of
our lives. The meshing of inner perceptions and outer experiences joined
with conscious awareness is an essentially spiritual way of living life. It
recognizes the innate creativity of life choices.

Women who choose abortion often achieve significant personal growth
because the creative essence of pregnancy is redirected. Pregnancy as a profound inner experience directs us to do this. Abortion conflicts plead with
us to pay attention to the organization of our inner world.

If a woman tries to isolate her experience of abortion from the rest of
her life she will find herself in a great deal of psychic pain. The extent of
her pain is likely to be in direct proportion to how much she isolates. As
she moves away from herself and others, she becomes subject to increasing
levels of discomfort that might interfere in her daily functioning.

The function of our internal emotional pain is to get our attention. It is an attempt on the part of our personal energy system—our consciousness operating on physical, mental, emotional, and spiritual levels—to encourage us to take a look at what is going on. As a woman turns towards herself, she might discover the need to explore how the decision she made about her pregnancy has made an impact on her life.

Most confusing for some women is the awareness that the process of making the decision to have an abortion was not thoroughly thought through. So much might have gone on unconsciously that a woman could feel like she was sleepwalking when she had her abortion. If that is the case, she will be left feeling bewildered as to "how I could have done that." Her struggle afterwards will be about becoming clear and present with herself about having had an abortion.

When a woman attends to her inner life around pregnancy and abortion, she is likely to find that it holds the power to offer a sense of connection to Life. Her sense of connection with another soul in pregnancy will often help to turn her in the direction of aligning herself with her purpose in the world. If she has had dreams or visions about the being from her pregnancy she might find that they contain messages about her life. If she remains open to receiving guidance from the messages she can learn a great deal.

Some women report that after an abortion the energy around the pregnancy being—the fetus, baby, or child—remains around them for a period of time. They say it feels like another consciousness or a presence of some kind. One woman referred to it as "my new friend." Another wondered if the being she had named and communicated with during pregnancy had not intended to come all the way through. Maybe its function was only to prod her to open to herself and live her life more honestly as she became more aware.

Spiritual Guidance

Spiritual experiences—the experiences of soul—are more common than we usually acknowledge. As we look for meaning and purpose in our lives, we can find ourselves dropping into a sense of being guided by a deeper knowing. We can count on the intuitive, nonjudgmental wisdom of the soul-self to give guidance in ways that are appropriate and nourishing for mental, physical, and emotional health. All that is required is to give respectful attention to the process, including events and insights that are emotionally or physically painful.

An abortion and the circumstances surrounding it can provide fertile ground for exploration of soul existence. When contradictory inner experiences surface at the time of a crisis pregnancy, they produce a vibrational tension in the body-mind-soul-spirit. The coexistence of societal and personal conflicts serves to pry open the pathways to deep emotion and contact with soul.

Once contact with soul is established, exploration of experiences in the physical plane takes on a decidedly different quality. We begin to think in terms of life lessons rather than hopeless categories of blaming. We want to confront our fears rather than run from them. We want to feel more rather than less, even if some of our feelings are painful.

One way to contact the soul is through truth telling. This is probably one of the ideas behind Catholic confession. But confession, as it has been practiced since the seventh century,[44] can backfire because it takes place in a context of restrictive power and punishment. The truth being told is subject to the judgment of church-defined truth, which assumes that everyone is born a "sinner."

Truth telling is most efficacious when the person speaking is held in a container of love and respect without judgment of any kind. It is a road to healing and empowerment if it is witnessed correctly. The fierce conflicts around abortion can create internal tension and pressure that can be alleviated only by revealing the truth to others. Many women feel propelled to search out and speak with friends and family who will listen with care. Sometimes a woman will have to reach beyond her normal circle to find the right support. As she does this she might discover the need to rearrange the oppressive conditions of her way of living.

Some women do this by becoming politically active. As painful as their abortion experiences might have been, they become vehement in their defense of legal abortion. Some women join with others in projects that benefit their communities. Others make changes in their close relationships, changes that reflect their newfound self-respect. Still others make geographic moves, start new careers, change jobs, or go back to school.

The spiritual aspect of our lives guides everything else. Spiritual growth is the process of becoming consciously aware of that guidance. It is learning to listen to inner guidance and to access information from the body. It is learning to be one with self and source. The process involves accessing the innate inner intelligence of our being. As we do this we recognize our connection to the Body-Mind-Soul-Spirit of Earth.

For a woman to realize her true self she must challenge and discard the ways of patriarchy. She cannot remain within the confines of male-centered definitions of woman if she wants to be a whole person. We must learn how to ground our awareness in our experience. We must learn how to define our experience in our own terms.

Women's spirituality is about developing and bringing through the non-patriarchal feminine aspects of self, the true self that is connected to the source of Life itself. It is about striving to be whole. The lesson of Spirit is ultimately about learning to be with Love, to be *At Love*, which means to open to loving and being loved.

The lesson of pregnancy is about learning to be with the body and the flow of sexual energy through the body. The meaning of the abortion experience is to allow women to make conscious life-centered choices that enhance our own lives and the lives of those around us.

Ultimately choosing for self and learning to express the true self is the most generous gift anyone can give to the world. It puts us in touch with our creativity and our passion for life—our ability to move creatively in the world.

The message of abortion in our time is that we as a society must change our patriarchal ways. As women learn to separate pregnancy and childbearing from our womanhood and personhood, we learn that we can choose the place of pregnancy in our lives. We are learning to choose how we want to have relationships—with children, with men, and with other women. We are learning that we can choose to fulfill ourselves as individual souls with individual creative purpose. Abortion with its complex of contentious issues and emotions plays a central and dramatic role in this for many women.

"Aborting Myself from Myself"

When I met Lili she'd had five abortions. The first one occurred when she was nineteen and in her first sexual relationship. She found herself isolated and alone afterwards, and unable to talk with anyone about what she had gone through. The other four abortions took place over the next ten years.

Now in her thirties and looking back over her experiences, Lili said that she had been "heartbroken and shocked" by the pregnancies, and locked in a cycle of "desperation, isolation, and frozenness." She went on:

> *Although rationally I had decided that I was not ready to have a child, I still felt a deep barrenness from having conceived, more than once, and quickly removing the little life from my body, my life.*

And:

> *I began to open to the feelings I had buried and considered dealt with, my feelings of sorrow and vulnerability. At first I only had a dim glimpse of the energy inside, and I thought I was either making it all up or that it would be all right just to leave be...time would heal all. The trauma was controlling me from the inside. It seemed as though*

in the place of babies I had given birth to rigid darkness and was abort-
ing my confidence in myself and relationships.

Lili said that the metaphor of abortion in her life was "how I aborted
myself from myself."

And so I'm healing the abortion and opening up to the actual physical
pain I've been feeling in my body from the pressure and heartfelt feel-
ings. I want to come back to myself. This is a very real metaphor for
me, to be able to do that through working with the abortion process,
to allow myself to feel the feelings that I have and not cut them off, and
to completely embody myself by being with the truth.

A solution for Lili was to organize support groups of other women who'd
had abortions. She was delighted that most of these women were anxious
to share their feelings. The process of bringing her inner life out in the open
allowed Lili to feel more alive. She noticed she could breathe more deeply
as her fears were aired, and said she felt "a transparent inner satisfaction"
as she came to know what she was like inside.

She learned much in the groups, and in her work on her own. By medi-
tating regularly she became practiced at looking inside herself for answers.

It turned out that I had the basic help I needed inside already, and to
insist that the solution was out there reinforced my sense of aborted trust
and inner deafness and rigidity.

As she learned to challenge her upbringing, which had taught her to re-
press her feelings, she found that she was "grateful for the depth of my emotional and perceptual devastation." She began to see that she had been
following a natural course of growth and healing and that the meaning it

had for her was giving her a new consciousness about the essence of her own true nature.

The Spiritual Dimension of Abortion

In an exchange in a post-abortion support group women had this to say about the spiritual dimension of life and of abortion:

Lana: To me the spiritual part is how your life functions, how you relate to life, how significant every little thing that you do all day long is; how interwoven everything is. It's hard to talk about. It's hard to find words to describe spiritual experiences. It's about discovering life in everything, that everything matters. It's respect for life.

Dawn: The spiritual dimension is that place where I have connected the most. I have an image of roots that are in the Earth and that give me nurturing and sustenance; and a circle of how all of us are connected in the world. It has to do with openness, an open heart, and receptivity and embracing. It's not a lofty thing; it's really earthy.

Lana: When I first found out I was pregnant I felt immense fear and guilt. I'm really taken with how powerful it is to be pregnant, to be able to bring a life into the world, that sexuality created it. To have a physical thing in your body that has a direct connection to infinity, to God; I mean it creates life! My heart will never be the same. It's connected to the moon, the stars, to everything!

Celie: When you first said spirituality and abortion, I thought, oh, they're not even connected. But then I got in touch with the incredible energy in pregnancy. I know how opening pregnancy can be, having gone through two pregnancies and having two children. Energy goes in and down when you're pregnant. There was a lot of combustible energy in letting go of that pregnancy. Something

changed that was different than if I hadn't been pregnant. I felt a
new love and joy in my life.

Dawn: I'm thinking about the process that I went through, about
praying to the spirit of the uterus to return to the universe, that
kind of surrender praying. I drew a picture for myself of the spirit
leaving the uterus.

The last session of the group was reserved for a ritual. Each woman
brought a different piece to the ceremony, including flowers, incense, photographs, and other objects of beauty, purification, and personal significance. Lili began:

*I wrote to the beings who came through me. I've also written to myself
and to all women. What I felt I needed to purify is my own clinging to
negative feelings, clinging to whatever has passed and that I need to let
go of it. I've never done this before, to actually send a sincere and genuine verbal message to all those. This is an important moment for me
to have you all together and be here:*

*"To you who have come to me so intimately and powerfully, I want
to acknowledge our eternal connection. I have the deepest feelings of
love and gratitude for you. You have brought me in touch with some
of the most important female feelings: unity, mercy, and love. I wasn't
able to keep you when you were alive, which I eternally regret. However,
I eternally send you love and wishes for your safety, health, strength,
and good fortune. I pray we will meet again."*

*To myself and all women who have made a decision to terminate
pregnancy:*

*"Let us have compassion and love for ourselves. Let us let go of cling-
ing to pain and guilt and self-punishment. Let us let go of these beings
also. Let us have the courage to go beyond our feelings of fear and lim-
itation, and to acknowledge our grief, sadness, and shock. May we let*

it go so that these feelings can deepen our compassion, but not torment us. It is a lesson in letting go, not only of possible children, but also of limited images of ourselves and others. May we learn from these experiences that life is change, not destruction. May we trust the invisible, the energies of love that come in and move out of our lives in different forms. May we open our hearts to communication in whatever form it comes to us, to allow ourselves to feel and let go—to experience and generate love for ourselves and all of life."

Then it was Dawn's turn. She showed us a photograph of her boyfriend, from whom she was receiving a great deal of love and support. She asked each of us to write our intentions and wishes on a piece of paper and then to burn them, "sending the energy out into the universe." She recited the words to a song:

Changing, changing
Ever changing
Like the phases of the moon
Changing, changing
Life is changing
Ever nearer, ever soon

There's a woman in the moon
I can see her when she's whole
When she's bright (she's the moon)
And deep as the sea
And soft
And strong
As can be[45]

Beyond Abortion

For what we have lost is the certainty that our planet will continue to support life. We now know in a way that humans have never known before that our lives are permeable, fragile, and delicately interwoven with all other life on this planet.

—SHERRY RUTH ANDERSON AND
PATRICIA HOPKINS, *THE FEMININE FACE OF GOD*

FOR WOMEN TO SAFELY AND PEACEFULLY DETERMINE THE flow of life through pregnancy, the dynamics of personal and societal power will have to change. We will have to move from inequality to equality and create opportunities for all people to develop their innate gifts. Equality of opportunity goes hand in hand with recognition of the wide diversity and talent among individuals, and a societal commitment to developing those talents. Recognition and respect for the unique individuality of each person in the context of community will have to replace competitive individualism.

To build a society based on human need, with love of all beings as its guiding principle, the reproductive needs of women have to be included in the center of the foundation. The feminine aspects of life, heretofore treated as peripheral, marginal, or unimportant, must be given their rightful status as central to the human condition.

Our economic system will have to change from private corporate profiteering to socialization and cooperation with an emphasis on the creative potential of both individuals and communities. There is no other way to establish true equality for all people, and without true equality women will not be able to step into our power as channels of Life. As women push the tide of history towards our full participation in the life of society, we can help to guide the organization of society towards less reliance on hierarchies of dominance and subordination.

The new economy will stabilize around a true and inclusive focus on the family and on humans caring for other humans. It would include high standards for the education of all children, universal health care, housing, employment, and the health of the environment, as well as issues of production.[46] No one will be left out. The needs of all will be considered, including the needs of the more than human community—the land, plants, and animals—with whom we share the Earth.

The political system will have to change, away from bureaucratic hierarchies to cooperative forms that allow people to consistently voice their needs and to learn constructive ways to get those needs met. These truly democratic and representative forms would promote participation by citizens in their communities rather than control by moneyed interests.

The medical system will have to change. An abortion, like giving birth, is an emotional, relational, and spiritual experience that takes place through the body. It is not mainly medical. The way most abortions are performed within the medical system denies and distorts the experience. Choosing to have an abortion is an expression of a woman's power in Life, but the medical system often reinforces the victimization of women by treating us as if we were being rescued. This is disempowering.

The techno-medical system in the United States dehumanizes people. Many of the services need to be demedicalized. Women's health clinics, and really all medical facilities, should be centered on the person seeking care—her education, her needs, and her point of view. Physicians should operate as equal members of teams of caregivers, and all health professionals should be trained in counseling skills.

Along with societal changes, the family will have to change, away from rigid, exclusive ways of organization to forms that recognize diversity among people and creative ways of living. Laws that enforce narrow definitions of family will need to be broadened to recognize the value of each family member. The family itself, with all its creative diversity, would be seen as an intrinsic part of community. The laws and practices of our communities would embrace all families and their needs. The educational system would provide everyone with instruction about emotional life and the nature of relationships, beginning in the lower grades.

Sexual morality will also have to change, away from attitudes and laws that limit or exploit human contact, to ways that foster contact based on openness, mutual respect, and recognition of individual differences.

People are learning to guide sexuality consciously. The shock of unintended pregnancies is often the catalyst that confronts us with the need to change the way we engage sexually. The drama that unfolds around abortion is a staging ground to become aware of how we express ourselves in the world—sexually and creatively. It gives us a chance to bring together our sexual and creative lives.

When the leaf of the mother plant is pinched the plant will reproduce itself in another part of itself or in another way. It dies into itself. People create themselves similarly. If a person closes off one possibility in Life another possibility opens. It is Nature's way.

The statement a woman makes when she makes a conscious choice in pregnancy represents the profound nature of the changes for all women at this time of history. It is a genuine piece of *herstory, yourstory, ourstory.*

The next step in human evolution is the establishment of conscious loving relationships based on respect and equality. Under these circumstances unwanted pregnancies will be rare. Until then, women will continue to carry the responsibility for life and make decisions about pregnancy. Abortion will continue to be one of these decisions until the lessons of the experiences are learned.

A great deal has to change before unwanted pregnancy and abortion become things of the past or occasional occurrences.

The day will come when the tide of technology turns towards birth control methods that are both completely safe and effective. A time will come when the energy of sexuality is liberated from the confusion of patriarchal, class, and racist judgments.

Women's lives will be different when communication with ourselves and with men about intimate sexual relations is clear and direct, when there is no such thing as rape, when our society supports children and their mothers in such a way that life is more than the predictable poverty of single parenthood, and when there is no such thing as an illegitimate child because all children are considered legitimate and valuable regardless of the circumstances of their birth.

Sexual intercourse between women and men will take place under conditions of heightened awareness of self in relationship. It will take place only when mutually desired, and pregnancy will occur only when the will and desire to have a child is present.

Most sexual activity will be for the purpose of self-creation in relationship and to give joyful energy to the world. Sexual relationships between people of the same sex will be unquestioned and common, and categories of heterosexuality and homosexuality will disappear. Gone as well will be divisions based on race and class, as these limiting categories of identity will have become irrelevant. Sexual exploitation for profit will no longer be part of society.

Fully conscious sexual activity depends upon being fully present in one's body. Being fully present in the body implies full mental contact with bodily functions. Mental interaction with bodily function will be able to occur naturally, mediated by the emotions. Through awareness of feelings, thoughts will be transmitted through and to the organs of the body. Mental and emotional awareness of all parts of bodily functions will serve to regulate the way in which physical events take place.

This being the case, the release of an egg from an ovary would take place at will instead of unconsciously, as is now the case. The use of self and body in creation would be the result of decision making on a soul level. The bringing through of another soul into physical form would occur through soul-to-soul communication. This communication would take place *before* the physical occurrence of pregnancy.

It could happen in one of two ways. Either a soul desiring to come into the physical would request the services of a woman, or a woman would make it known that she is available and willing to bring through a soul to the physical. No pregnancies would occur other than those agreed upon in such a way. Amy Shapiro puts it this way:

> In a society more capable of understanding the Spirit/Matter relationship, we would enter into loving dialogue with the inherently wise intelligence of our body's cells, including the ovaries, ova and sperm. Women would encourage their bodies either to conceive or to abstain from conception, with the introduction of sperm. Men would "steer" their sperm to penetrate or refrain from penetrating the ovum. In an ideal state of mind-body relatedness, a woman would "program" her uterus to prepare for implantation, if desired, or to miscarry an unwanted pregnancy.[47]

All this presupposes a different society and collective consciousness than the one in which we live now. It is not possible to say how much longer it will take for humankind to evolve to this point. Free, conscious sexuality requires freedom and safety in the physical environment. Responsibility for self in relationship can take place only under circumstances of respect, safety, and security. All basic physical requirements—food, shelter, health, and beauty—must be provided to allow human relationships to flower.

The necessary social and economic changes will have to be worldwide to provide safety for all people to engage in self-fulfilling, loving relationships. This will require abolishing economic activities that profit from human need. The global economy would instead be organized to provide needed goods and services, and regulated according to the needs of all people everywhere.

We must bring our human intelligence and compassionate judgment to bear on the nature and quality of Life on Earth. The planet needs our loving attention. All the technology in the world will not release us from our fundamental responsibility to be in right relationship with the world, with all living beings, and especially with each other.

The process of bringing conscious awareness to bear on decisions about pregnancy is a natural function of women. The power of the female body and consciousness is part of Nature just as all of human nature is part of Nature. Women's life-giving power includes death sometimes. Abortion kills as frost and lightning kill, or avalanches, or earthquakes. Mountains, rivers, deserts, forests, and oceans take responsibility for themselves by returning to balance after great disturbances.

Abortion for some women is experienced as a natural disaster. For others it is a blessing. For some it is both. The movement of natural forces such as earth, wind, fire, and water brings about right relationship in nature. Right relationship for human beings depends upon conscious awareness of our environment and of ourselves. Intelligent, loving attentiveness can be brought to our relationships with everyone and everything in our lives. When women take themselves and their choice-making seriously their choices are made respectfully.

To be respectful towards Life means to take responsibility for our part in it. This is what we do when we make choices in pregnancy. As we come to respect and love ourselves and let go of shame-based attitudes, we can embrace our sexuality as part of the core of ourselves.

Men are changing, too. As they are freed from their role as dominator they will find their human tenderness and live their lives accordingly. A man will no longer believe he is not a real man if he expresses his emotions. He will no longer have to be ready to do battle. War as an instrument of domination and greed will be abolished. Sexuality will never be channeled violently.

Decisions about pregnancy engage our hearts and souls. It is natural that they do. As a woman exercises her power to create life she is given a glimpse of her wholeness. The power of pregnancy lies in its capacity to empower a woman on a spiritual level. It allows her to embody herself. It brings Nature and Spirit together, and puts her in touch with the natural ebb and flow of relationships in Life.

Healing the pain of abortion has to do with the development of the individual and with nurturing the development of the person towards wholeness. It is about women developing as whole people. Abortion must be treated in ways that enhance and protect the integrity of the individual and the movement towards wholeness. Vital to this is the development of openheartedness in human beings, individually and collectively—openheartedness towards life, towards death, and towards everything in between.

We must adopt a transformational attitude towards abortion centered in women's experience. The power to bring forth life, embodied in women, includes the power to say yes and the power to say no. As this power is affirmed and strengthened by women and by society, the number of unintended and unwanted pregnancies will gradually decline. At this stage of history, choosing abortion for some pregnancies is an exercise by women of our moral responsibility—to ourselves as individuals reaching and searching for wholeness, to others in our immediate circle of love relations, and to the human family and Life on this planet.

APPENDIX 1: HEALING TOOLS

Some of the exercises and suggestions that follow are for women who have already had abortions. Some are for women who are considering having an abortion, and some are for women who have decided. Some of the exercises work well when done with a partner or friend. Please use them in whatever ways they seem helpful to you.

BREATHE AND CENTER

The simplest way to bring your focus to yourself and control anxiety is to concentrate on your breathing. Breathing in a conscious way allows you to focus on your thoughts and feelings without feeling afraid. It allows you to relax into yourself and be present with your sensory experience. Conscious breathing can be done anywhere and at any time under most circumstances.

Sit comfortably or stand in such a way that you are balanced on your legs and feet. Take a deep breath through your nose and let it out slowly through your mouth. Do that two or three more times. When you exhale, be sure to release all the air before you take another breath. Each time you breathe in and out notice where you are holding tension in your body. When you exhale, let go of the tension in your body. Be sure to breathe slowly and naturally. Breathe this way until you feel a clear shift in your level of relaxation.

Continue to be aware of your breathing as you close your eyes and center deep inside yourself. Locate the center of your being. Breathe into that center and remain focused there. Let your mind clear. Stay in that centered state for as long as it feels natural to do so. Out of your centeredness you will be able to approach the tasks of your life and any decision making with more ease, steadiness, and clarity.

SPEND TIME IN NATURE

It is helpful to spend time in natural surroundings when dealing with issues of pregnancy and the flow of the life process. We see the cycles of life-death-life most clearly in this environment. Take yourself to a place where you can spend some uninterrupted time among trees, rocks, and other growing things. This may be a wilderness area, city park, botanical garden, or back yard. It may be a lake, river, or ocean. Go there with a clear intention and allow yourself to feel the energies of the nonhuman living beings around you. Write your intention in your journal. Write down any questions you have about your experience with pregnancy or abortion. Observe the natural world around you, above you, and below you. Pay particular attention to the sky. Notice what answers and solutions come to you from your observations. Write or draw what comes to you.

CONNECT WITH THE EARTH

Sit in a place outside that feels comfortable and comforting. You might want to lean against a friendly tree or lie on a big rock or sit in the middle of a meadow. Feel the Earth beneath you. Tell yourself that the planet supports you to make whatever choice you have made or are about to make about pregnancy. Let whatever fear you are carrying dissolve into the Earth. Close your eyes and feel your core connecting to the core of the Earth. Feel the power there. Relax into it. Take a ride on the Earth as it rotates on its axis and travels around the sun. Write in your journal about any thoughts, feelings, images, or associations that come to you.

CONNECT WITH YOUR BODY

Find a quiet place to sit or lie down comfortably. Use your intuition to choose a good place to be. Prepare your body by gently stretching and bending while breathing before you settle down in one place. Be sure you are not hungry or tired when you do this. Allow about an hour for this time with your body. You might enjoy listening to relaxing music to support this exercise.

Breathe and center. Close your eyes and continue breathing slowly and evenly. Scan your body with your mind. Notice any places in your body where tension is being held. Release the tension from those places when you exhale.

Focus your awareness inside your body. Ask if there is a part of your body that would like some attention or that you sense is calling you. Go there with your awareness. Ask that part of your body for any information it has for you about choices you have made or are making. Listen carefully with your inner intelligence. Allow for silences. Stay open to whatever information is coming your way.

When you feel finished, bring your awareness back to your breathing. When you are ready, open your eyes. Thank your body for its wisdom. Write in your journal about any thoughts, feelings, images, or associations that came to you.

SIT WITH YOUR ABORTION

Sit and focus on the word *abortion*. On a large sheet of paper, with whatever drawing materials you have, draw whatever designs or images come to you. Write in your journal about what you have drawn. Include how it felt to make the drawing and your feelings and thoughts about the images you have created.

WORDSTORM

You can create a wordstorm by writing down all the words you can think of that are associated with a particular word or subject. It is most effective if it is done as quickly as possible in a stream of consciousness manner. It's fun when done by a group of women together. The following are words and phrases associated with the word *abortion* that came from some of the women in abortion support groups I have led.

Relief, fear, confusion, being pregnant, spirit of the baby, fetus, tears, sadness, choices, empowerment, relationships, family issues, religion, blood, body, end of childbearing time, pain, closeness to nature, isolation, grief, shock, surprise, feeling alone, personal morality, difficult circumstances, life, death, responsibility, guilt, blaming the victim, control over our lives, more than one abortion, children, unexpected experience, anger, abortion politics, patriarchy, men, sex, birth control, personal searching, control, shame, mothering, doctors, medical issues, health, secrets, telling parents, relating to children, inner child issues, pregnancy fantasies, what ifs, judgments about self, abortion medical procedure, body vulnerability, no real choices in society, loss of soul, violation, significant life passage, saying no to birth, sex education, babies, women.

Make your own list of words and phrases. Do some writing about one or more of them.

DECIDING ABOUT A PREGNANCY

If you are not sure in what direction you want to go with a current pregnancy, you might be feeling anxious because you think you have to make a decision quickly. If it feels like life is moving too fast, focus on slowing it down. Pretend you have all the time in the world. Calm down. Say to yourself, *I am the best person to make a decision about this pregnancy. I will make my decision to the best of my ability as soon as I can.*

Since time is often an issue when abortion is being considered, it might help if you set a deadline for your decision. You could tell yourself you will have your mind made up in one week or two weeks. Set a definite date for the decision to be final, and mark it in your calendar. Then, relax into the time you have set and allow yourself to do what you need to do to make the decision.

Do you need more information? What information do you need? Make lists. Make phone calls. Search the Internet. Go to the library and read about pregnancy. If you are considering adoption, call adoption agencies. If you are considering being a single parent, call social service agencies in your area and find out what the resources are. If you would like to know more about the cost of maternity care, call a local hospital, gynecologist, or midwife. If you want to know more about abortion, call clinics or private doctors that provide abortion services. These can be found in the phone book or online.

Think of who you need to talk to and talk to them. Seek out support. You don't have to be in this alone. A pregnancy crisis is easier to deal with when you involve those close to you. It's more scary and stressful when you deny yourself support. Ask people for help and let them help you. Think about whom it is you would like to talk with. Is it your boyfriend? Your husband? Your parents? A sister or brother? A cousin? A teacher in your school? Your minister or rabbi? A good friend?

Talking with a private counselor or psychotherapist might be another way for you to receive help and support as you clarify your decision. Pregnancy decision counseling is available at many women's health centers and Planned Parenthood clinics. Open-minded or pro-choice members of the clergy might be available in your area as well.

Take good care of yourself physically when you are in the process of making your decision. Pregnancy often produces symptoms of fatigue and nausea because of the surge of hormones in the body during the first twelve weeks. Rest when you need to; drink lots of water; and eat as healthily as possible. Vitamin and mineral supplements can be helpful. Check with a nutritionist or herbalist about whether this is a good idea for you. Take walks as a way to move your body, and give yourself time to think while you're walking.

THINKING IN A CIRCLE

This decision making exercise is a little more elaborate.

Make a circle on the floor with rocks, seeds, cloth, or other materials you have around. Make it large enough for you to be able to sit comfortably in the center of it. Place a candle at each of the four directions—south, west, north, and east. Along the inside edge of the circle, place objects of significance to you in your decision about your pregnancy. An object of significance is anything that represents an aspect of your life. Significant objects may include photographs, books, clothing, equipment, tools, jewelry, stuffed animals, rocks, crystals, artwork, your journal, family heirlooms, musical instruments, and the like. Allow yourself to be freely guided by your intuition as you put things in their places. There is no right way or wrong way to do this—only your way.

Sit in the center of the circle. Light the candles. Call in the power of Nature by calling in the four directions. Turn and face each direction. Feel the energy there. Move clockwise around the directions. Your choice to begin in the south, west, north, or east will be made according to what feels right to you. Sing or chant if a song or chant comes to you.

Turn and face each object you have placed in the circle. Speak to it (out loud if you wish) and listen to it. Allow it to speak to you. Ask for help about the direction you are considering for the pregnancy.

Take your time. This process may take a while. You may complete it in an hour or you might want to stretch it over a few days. Keep a record of what comes up for you as you move through it. Write in your journal or speak into a recorder as you go along.

FOCUS ON THE POSITIVES

This, too, is for decision making.

Divide a piece of paper in three columns if you are also considering adoption. Head the first column *Have the baby and keep it*, the second, *Have the baby and give it up for adoption*, and the third, *Have an abortion*. Pick any of the three columns to start with, and stay with that column until you can't think of anything else to write there. Then move to the next column.

List all the *good* things you can think of about each option, moving from one to the other only after you can't think of anything else. Staying with the positives will help you to see more clearly and with less fear what might lie ahead with each of the three possible choices in pregnancy. You may feel different on different days, so repeat this exercise on different days until you feel clearer about the issues that come up.

PICTURE YOUR LIFE

And this is also for decision making.

Draw a picture or diagram of the way your life looks to you now. Include the main activities in your life such as work, school, family, volunteer commitments, community projects, sports, the arts, and other hobbies and interests that take up your time. Include important people such as friends and family members. Also, include your living situation.

On another sheet of paper draw a picture or diagram of how your life might look with each of the possible choices in pregnancy. Use a separate piece of paper for each choice. When you are done, put all the drawings on the wall. Study them over the next few days. Note your insights.

CREATE A HEALING CIRCLE

Bring together a small group of women you know to help you face and express your thoughts and feelings about having an abortion. Begin by holding hands and feeling the energy of the circle. Then, speak about what has been happening to you and ask the women to support you as you go through it. You might want them to simply witness or you might also want them to reflect back to you what they are seeing and hearing from you. The ritual you create will depend on who you are and what you need as well as who the other women are and what they have to offer.

MORE JOURNAL WRITING IDEAS

Write the story of your abortion. If you have had more than one abortion, write the story of each experience. If you find yourself resistant to doing this, try writing in the third person as though you were writing about someone else. Be as detailed as possible in your writing. If writing is not appealing to you, tell your story into a recorder instead.

Write about any of the topics in the wordstorm exercise.

Write a letter to the fetus/baby/child explaining why you decided to have an abortion. Say everything you need to say.

Write a letter to someone to whom you need to express your thoughts and feelings about your abortion. You may or may not want to mail the letter. Express yourself freely.

Speak or write directly to Spirit/God/Goddess/Creator about your abortion experience.

Write a letter to yourself about your abortion. Say everything you need to say. If you have difficulty being compassionate towards yourself, pretend you are writing to another person.

PREPARING FOR AN ABORTION

If you have decided to have an abortion, here are some suggestions about how to make arrangements for the medical procedure.

Get as much information as possible before you go in for an appointment for an abortion. Call around to different clinics, hospitals, or doctors' offices. Find out which ones provide abortion services in your area. Or, if you have to travel for services, how that works. Ask them to explain their philosophy of care and exactly how they provide the abortion services. For example, do they give you someone to talk with who will answer questions and describe what is going to happen?

Here are other questions:

- What is the medical procedure for abortion? Is it medicine or surgery?
- Do they use local or general anesthesia?
- Are prescription medications included in the cost of the abortion?
- What are the risks and complications of abortion?
- Do they provide a counselor to accompany you during the abortion procedure?
- Do they provide medical follow-up care?

- What do they do in case of medical emergency?
- Who is the practitioner who will be performing the medical procedure? What is her/his experience?
- Is it okay to bring a friend along with you when you go there for your appointment?
- How long can you expect to be at the facility when you go for your appointment?
- Do they have anti-abortion picketers at their facility?

The abortion medical procedure facilitates the change from being pregnant to not being pregnant. *Do not* have the medical procedure done until you have let go or are ready to begin to earnestly let go of the pregnancy in your mind. If you hold onto the pregnancy emotionally and mentally during the physical process of an abortion, your experience will likely be filled with the stress of your mental resistance to ending the pregnancy, and you might have more physical pain.

Try not to suppress your feelings about letting go of the pregnancy. Be fully in touch with your feelings. If you feel sadness and loss about ending the pregnancy, let yourself feel what you feel. At the same time, be fully in touch with your decision to end the pregnancy and allow an internal dialogue to develop within you so that you can instruct your body to let go of the pregnancy.

Be an active participant in your abortion. Develop a working relationship with the practitioner who will perform the procedure. Sometimes this is not possible, as many medical facilities and doctors are not oriented to allow this to happen. If it is not possible, you might still remain in control of your part of the procedure. Verbally communicate with the staff of the clinic about how you are feeling and what you need. This might be difficult if you are not accustomed to doing this. Remember, you have a right to ask for what you need.

Most facilities expect you to fit into their system of operation. Find out the details of their system. Ask a lot of questions. Negotiate with them so that you feel as safe and secure as possible about receiving good care. Play an active role in your abortion. Don't assume. Ask. Remember, you are probably feeling more vulnerable than usual.

This does not translate into being hostile or confrontational. You don't need to take a fighting stance. Most of the counselors, nurses, and doctors who work in abortion facilities do so because they are devoted to providing choices in pregnancy for women. They are serving women. The best of them are sensitive to the crisis nature of the experience and try to be flexible about differences in needs among individuals.

You are in charge of your experience. You are engaging the services of medical and counseling professionals to help you to have an abortion. They are not doing anything *to* you. Use your abortion as an opportunity to empower yourself. Use it as a chance to assert yourself as an individual woman in charge of her own life. Take a deep breath and blow away all your fear and confusion. Know that you can handle what is happening to you.

GET INVOLVED IN YOUR COMMUNITY

Having an abortion might make you aware of yourself and society in ways you had not anticipated. You might feel and see things differently. Having an abortion often raises questions about the way we are living our lives and the way society is organized. One of the best ways to heal your emotional pain is to help other people. After you have spent some time focusing on your personal situation, you may find you want to look outward and find ways to apply your interests and skills to help others.

Many communities have clearing houses or centers for volunteers to be placed in agencies. If you contact one of these, you can be guided towards different possibilities for you to make a contribution.

SEEK PROFESSIONAL HELP

Counseling with a professional counselor or psychotherapist could be a good choice for you if the circumstances of your life are such that you are unable to get any relief from your emotional pain. You could benefit from counseling if your abortion experience has triggered other issues in your life and you are having difficulty sorting it all out. If your pregnancy resulted from sexual assault or sexual abuse by someone in your family, it could be important for you to find a good counselor or psychotherapist to talk with.

Choose your counselor or psychotherapist carefully. Think about the qualities that you would like that person to have and what you need in counseling. Make a list of questions to ask the counselor in an initial interview. Be assertive about what you need to know. You are hiring this person to help you to know yourself better and to support you to make changes.

If you are not sure how to find a good counselor, call a local women's health center or Planned Parenthood clinic and ask them to recommend someone. You might have to make a number of phone calls because someone refers you to someone who refers you to someone else. Don't be discouraged if you don't find someone right away.

Additional Reading

Books can be extraordinarily transformative as well as informative. Here are some titles that helped me to write this book and that I heartily recommend.

WOMEN'S STUDIES AND PSYCHOLOGY (CLASSIC WORKS)

Toward A New Psychology of Women, Jean Baker Miller
In A Different Voice, Carol Gilligan
Of Woman Born: Motherhood as Experience and Institution, Adrienne Rich

NATURE

Sisters of the Earth: Women's Prose and Poetry About Nature, editor, Lorraine Anderson
Woman and Nature: The Roaring Inside Her, Susan Griffin
Mother Nature: A History of Mothers, Infants, and Natural Selection, Sarah Blaffer Hrdy
The Four Shields: The Initiatory Seasons of Human Nature, Steven Foster with Meredith Little

SPIRITUALITY

The Feminine Face of God: The Unfolding of the Sacred in Women, Sherry Ruth Anderson and Patricia Hopkins
Women in Praise of the Sacred: 43 Centuries of Spiritual Poetry by Women, editor, Jane Hirshfield
Soul Contracts, Linda Baker

WOMEN'S HEALTH AND ABORTION HEALING

Our Bodies, Ourselves: A New Edition for a New Era, The Boston Women's Health
  Book Collective
Peace After Abortion, Ava Torre-Bueno
The Healing Choice: Your Guide to Emotional Recovery After an Abortion, Candace
  De Puy and Dana Dovitch
Pregnancy Options Workbook, Margaret R. Johnston
A Guide to Emotional and Spiritual Resolution After an Abortion, the creators of
  the *Pregnancy Options Workbooks*
*A Time to Decide, A Time to Heal: For parents making difficult decisions about babies
  they love*, Molly A. Minnick, Kathleen J. Delp, and Mary C. Ciotti

HISTORY

The Creation of Patriarchy, Gerda Lerner
The Creation of Feminist Consciousness, Gerda Lerner
Abortion and Woman's Choice: The State, Sexuality, and Reproductive Freedom,
  Rosalind Pollack Petchesky
Woman's Body, Woman's Right, Linda Gordon

Websites

www.earthskycounseling.com Describes my counseling and vision quest work.
www.lifechoicesteachingsofabortion.com The website and blog for this book.
www.pregnancyoptions.info Provides a wealth of information about all aspects
  of pregnancy choices, including links to other resources. The Pregnancy Options Workbook provides grounded, heartfelt support to address personal
  questions and issues.
www.ourbodiesourselves.org An important resource on women's health by the
  Boston Women's Health Book Collective, creators of the classic book, Our
  Bodies, Ourselves.
www.peaceafterabortion.com: Information about Ava Torre-Bueno's excellent
  book Peace After Abortion.
www.4exhale.org Exhale is a nonprofit, "pro-voice" hotline for women, their
  partners and families to receive support after abortion.
www.yourbackline.org Provides a forum to discuss "the broad range of experiences and emotions surrounding pregnancy, parenting, adoption and abortion."

www.prochoice.org The National Abortion Federation is the organization of abortion providers in the United States.

www.abortioncarenetwork.org The ACN describes itself as "a network of independent abortion providers, allies, and individuals who provide quality care for women," and that is "the driving force behind the movement to de-stigmatize and normalize the abortion experience while offering support and training to the abortion care community."

www.feministnetwork.org FAN "supports the continued success, excellence, and strength of feminist health care providers."

www.catholicsforchoice.org "Catholics for Choice (CFC) was founded in 1973 to serve as a voice for Catholics who believe that the Catholic tradition supports a woman's moral and legal right to follow her conscience in matters of sexuality and reproductive health."

www.rcrc.org The Religious Coalition for Reproductive Rights was founded in 1973 "to safeguard the newly won constitutional right to abortion."

www.nwhn.org The National Women's Health Network.

www.rhrealitycheck.org "RH Reality Check is an online community and publication serving individuals and organizations committed to advancing sexual and reproductive health and rights."

BIBLIOGRAPHY

Adler, Nancy E., et al, "Psychological Responses After Abortion," *Science*, vol. 248, April 1990.

Akwesasne Notes, ed., *Basic Call to Consciousness*. Summertown, TN: Book Publishing Company, 1995. Orig. pub. 1978.

Anderson, Lorraine, ed. *Sisters of the Earth: Women's Prose and Poetry About Nature*, New York: Vintage Books, 1991.

Anderson, Sherry Ruth, and Patricia Hopkins, *The Feminine Face of God: The Unfolding of the Sacred in Women*. New York: Bantam, 1991.

Bachrach, Christine A., Kathy Shepherd Stolley, and Kathryn A. London, "Relinquishment of Premarital Births: Evidence from National Survey Data," *Family Planning Perspectives*, vol. 24, no. 1, January/February, 1992.

Baehr, Ninia, *Abortion Without Apology: A Radical History for the 1990s*. Boston: South End Press, 1990. South End Press pamphlet no. 8.

Baker, Anne, *The Complete Book of Problem Pregnancy Counseling*. The Hope Clinic for Women, 1985.

Baker, Linda, *Abortion –A Spiritual Approach*. Audio cassette, 1991. Guided meditation.

————, *Soul Contracts*. Expanded edition, iUniverse, 2003. Orig. pub. Patchwork Press, 1998.

Baldwin, Christina, *Calling the Circle*. Mill Spring, NC: Swan-Raven & Co., 1994.

Barbach, Lonnie, *For Yourself: The Fulfillment of Female Sexuality*. New York: Doubleday/ Anchor Books, 1981.

Beard, Mary, *Woman as a Force in History*. New York: Collier (MacMillan), 1971. Orig. pub. 1946.

Beck, Renee, and Sydney Barbara Metrick, *The Art of Ritual*. Berkeley, CA: Celestial Arts 1990.

Beresford, Terry, *Short Term Relationship Counseling*. Planned Parenthood of Maryland, 1977.

Blank, Joani, and Marcia Quackenbush, *A Kid's First Book About Sex*. Burlingame, CA: Yes Press (Down There Press), 1983.

Boston Women's Health Book Collective, *Our Bodies, Ourselves: A New Edition for a New Era*. New York: Touchstone, 2005. Orig. pub. as *Our Bodies, Ourselves*, 1969.

Cassell, Carol, *Swept Away*. New York: Simon & Schuster, 1984.

Conscience magazine, Catholics for Choice, www.catholicsforchoice.org.

Chalker, Rebecca, and Carol Downer, *A Woman's Book of Choices*. New York: Four Walls Eight Windows, 1992.

Close, Henry T., "A Funeral Service for an Aborted Baby," *Voices*, Spring, 1988.

Davis, Angela Y., *Women, Race & Class*, New York: Vintage, 1981.

Davis, Nanette J., *From Crime to Choice: The Transformation of Abortion in America*. Westport CT: Greenwood Press, 1985.

DeBeauvoir, Simone, *The Second Sex*. New York: Vintage Books, 1974. Orig. pub. in France, 1949.

De Puy, Candance and Dana Dovitch, *The Healing Choice: Your Guide to Emotional Recovery After an Abortion*. New York: Fireside, 1997.

Eggebroten, Anne, ed., *Abortion—My Choice, God's Grace: Christian Women Tell Their Stories*. Pasadena, CA: New Paradigm Books, 1994.

Ehrenreich, Barbara, and Deirdre English, *For Her Own Good: 150 Years of the Experts Advice to Women*. New York: Anchor, 1978.

Ehrenreich, Barbara, "The Woman Behind the Fetus," *New York Times*, April 28, 1989.

Eichenbaum, Luise, and Susie Orbach, *What Do Women Want*. New York: Berkley Books, 1983.

Eisler, Riane, *The Chalice and the Blade*. San Francisco: Harper & Row, 1987.

Engels, Frederick, *The Origin of the Family, Private Property and the State*. Edited with Introduction by Eleanor Burke Leacock. New York: International Pub., 1972, 1985. Orig. pub. 1884.

Folbre, Nancy, *The Invisible Heart: Economics and Family Values*. New York: The New Press, 2001.

Foster, Steven, and Meredith Little, *The Four Shields: The Initiatory Seasons of Human Nature*. Lost Borders Press, 1998.

Gardner, Joy, *A Difficult Decision*. Freedom, CA: The Crossing Press, 1986.

Gardner, Kay, *Changing*, on *Mooncircles*. Audio cassette. Urana Records, 1975.

Gilligan, Carol, *In A Different Voice*. Cambridge, MA: Harvard University Press, 1982.

Gordon, Linda, *Woman's Body, Woman's Right*. New York: Penguin Books, 1977. Orig. pub. 1976.

Griffin, Susan, *Woman and Nature: The Roaring Inside Her*, New York: Harper & Row, 1977.

Gryte, Marilyn, *Inner Healing After Abortion*. mgryteinnerhealing.com. 1995, revised 2006.

Hardin, Garrett, "Some Biological Insights Into Abortion," *BioScience*, vol. 32, no. 9.

Harrison, Beverly Wildung, *Our Right to Choose*. Boston: Beacon Press, 1983.

Herman, Judith Lewis, *Trauma and Recovery*. Basic Books, 1992.

Hillman, James, *The Soul's Code: In Search of Character and Calling*. New York: Warner Books, 1996.

Hirschfield, Jane, ed., *Women in Praise of the Sacred: 43 Centuries of Spiritual Poetry by Women*, New York: HarperCollins, 1994.

hooks, bell, *Sisters of the Yam: Black Women and Self-Recovery*. Cambridge, MA: South End Press, 1993.

————, *Feminism is for Everybody: Passionate Politics*. Cambridge, MA: South End Press, 2000.

Hrdy, Sarah Blaffer, *Mother Nature: A History of Mothers, Infants, and Natural Selection*. New York: Pantheon Books, 1999.

Hull, N.E.H., and Peter Charles Hoffer, *Roe v. Wade: The Abortion Rights Controversy in American History*. Lawrence, KS: University Press of Kansas, 2001.

Iglehart, Hallie, *Womanspirit: A Guide to Women's Wisdom*. San Francisco: Harper & Row, 1983.

Ingerman, Sandra, *Soul Retrieval: Mending the Fragmented Self*. New York: Harper Collins, 1991.

James, Walene, "Abortion's Third Side: The Evidence," *At The Crossroads*, issue 3, December 1993.

Johnston, Margaret R., *Pregnancy Options Workbook*. Distributed by Ferre Institute, 124 Front St., Binghamton, NY 13905, (607) 724-4308 © 1998, revised in 1999, 2002, 2006, 2009.

————, and Terry Sallas Merritt, *A Guide to Emotional and Spiritual Resolution After an Abortion*. The Ferre Institute, 124 Front St., Binghamton, NY 13905. 2008, reprinted 2009. www.pregnancyoptionsinfo.

Jordan, Judith V., Alexandra G. Kaplan, Jean Baker Miller, Irene P. Stiver, and Janet L. Surrey, *Women's Growth In Connection*. New York: The Guilford Press, 1991.

Joy, Stephany Stone, "Abortion: An Issue to Grieve?" *Journal of Counseling and Development*, vol. 63, February, 1985.

Klassen, Albert D., Colin J. Williams, and Eugene E. Levitt, *Sex and Morality in the United States: An Empirical Inquiry Under the Auspices of the Kinsey Institute.* Edited by Hubert J. O'Gorman. Middletown, CT: Wesleyan University Press, 1989.

Lerner, Gerda, *The Creation of Patriarchy.* New York: Oxford University Press, 1986.

———, *The Creation of Feminist Consciousness.* New York: Oxford University Press, 1993.

Levine, Stephen, *Healing Into Life and Death.* New York: Anchor (Doubleday), 1987.

Luker, Kristin, *Taking Chances: Abortion and the Decision Not to Contracept.* Berkeley, CA: University of California Press, 1975.

———, *Abortion and the Politics of Motherhood.* Berkeley, CA: University of California Press, 1984.

Lunneborg, Patricia, *Abortion: A Positive Decision.* New York: Bergin and Garvey, 1992.

McDonnell, Kathleen, *Not An Easy Choice.* Boston: South End Press, 1984.

Maguire, Marjorie Reiley, and Daniel C., "Abortion: A Guide to Making Ethical Choices," *Conscience*, vol. IV, no. 5, September 1983.

Masters, William H., Virginia E. Johnson, and Robert C. Kolodny, *Masters and Johnson On Sex and Human Loving.* Boston: Little, Brown, and Company, 1985. Second Edition.

Miller, Jean Baker, *Toward a New Psychology of Women.* Boston: Beacon Press, 1986, Second Edition.

Minnick, Molly A., Delp, Kathleen J., Ciotti, Mary C., *A Time to Decide, A Time to Heal.* 4th edition. St. Johns, MI: Pineapple Press, P.O. Box 312, St. Johns, MI 48879, 2000.

Miller, Patricia G., *The Worst of Times.* New York: Harper-Collins, 1993.

Mohr, James C., *Abortion in America.* New York: Oxford University Press, 1978.

Morlock, Grace, "The Meaning of Abortion." Unpublished Masters thesis, Boulder Graduate School, Boulder, Colorado, 1990.

Morowitz, Harold J., and James S. Trefill, *The Facts of Life.* New York: Oxford University Press, 1992.

Napier, Nancy, *Sacred Practices for Conscious Living.* New York: W.W. Norton & Co., 1997.

Nathanson, Sue, *Soul Crisis: One Woman's Journey Through Abortion to Renewal.* New York: New American Library, 1989.

Noddings, Nel, *Caring: A Feminine Approach to Ethics and Moral Education.* Berkeley, CA: University of California Press, 1984.

Orbach, Susie, *Hunger Strike*. Avon Books, 1986.

Panuthos, Claudia, and Catherine Romeo, *Ended Beginnings: Healing Childbearing Losses*. South Hadley, MA: Bergin & Garvey, 1984.

Paris, Ginette, *The Sacrament of Abortion*. Dallas, TX: Spring Publications, 1992.

Petchesky, Rosalind Pollack, *Abortion and Woman's Choice: The State, Sexuality, and Reproductive Freedom*. Boston: Northeastern University Press, 1984.

Plotkin, Bill, *Nature and the Human Soul*. Novato, CA: New World Library, 2008.

Reardon, David C., *Aborted Women: Silent No More*. Chicago: Loyola University Press, 1987.

Retl, Irene, ed., *Childless By Choice: A Feminist Anthology*. Santa Cruz, CA: Her-Books, 1992.

Rich, Adrienne, *Of Woman Born: Motherhood as Experience and Institution*. New York: Bantam, 1976.

Rosenberg, Rosalind, *Divided Lives: American Women in the Twentieth Century*. New York: The Noonday Press, 1992.

Rothman, Barbara Katz, *The Tentative Pregnancy*. New York: Viking, 1986.

———, *Recreating Motherhood*. New York: W.W. Norton, 1989.

Sachdev, Paul, ed., *International Handbook on Abortion*. New York: Greenwood Press, 1988.

Schambelan, Bo, ed., *Roe v. Wade: The Complex Text of the Official U.S. Supreme Court Decision*. Philadelphia, PA: Running Press, 1992.

Schweickart, David, *After Capitalism*. Lanham, MD: Rowman & Littlefield, 2002.

Shapiro, Amy, "'Pro-Love' and the Ensoulement Dilemma," *The Journal of Regression Therapy*, vol. VI, no. 1, December 1992.

Sherfey, Mary Jane, *The Nature and Evolution of Female Sexuality*. New York: Vintage Books, 1972.

Singer, June, *Boundaries of the Soul*. Garden City, NY: Anchor Books, 1973.

Smith, Ellen, *Abortion and Personal Healing*. Unpublished paper for senior project, Naropa Institute, Boulder, CO, 1988.

Starhawk, *Dreaming the Dark*. Boston: Beacon Press, 1982.

Steinem, Gloria, *Revolution From Within: A Book of Self-Esteem*. Boston: Little, Brown and Company, 1992.

Solinger, Rickie, *Abortion Wars: A Half Century of Struggle, 1950-2000*. Berkeley, CA: University of California Press, 1998.

———, *Beggars and Choosers: How the Politics of Choice Shapes Adoption, Abortion, and Welfare in the United States*. New York: Hill and Wang, 2001.

Spitz, Rabbi Elie Kaplan, *Does the Soul Survive? A Jewish Journey to Belief in Afterlife, Past Lives & Living with Purpose*. Woodstock, VT: Jewish Lights, 2001.

Tavris, Carol, "Do Codependency Theories Explain Women's Unhappiness—or Exploit Their Insecurities?" *Vogue,* December 1989.

Torre-Bueno, Ava, *Peace After Abortion.* San Diego, CA: Pimpernel Press, 1996.

Townsend, Rita, and Ann Perkins, *Bitter Fruit: Women's Experiences of Unplanned Pregnancy, Abortion, and Adoption.* Alameda, CA: Hunter House, 1992.

Tworkov, Helen, "Anti-abortion/Pro-choice: Taking Both Sides," *Tricycle: The Buddhist Review,* Spring 1992.

Wade, Roger, *For Men About Abortion.* Pamphlet, Boulder, CO, 1978.

Wambach, Helen, *Life Before Life.* New York: Bantam, 1979.

Weber, Linda, *Healing the Pain of Abortion: An Exploration of the Psychology of Women.* Unpublished Master's thesis, Vermont College of Norwich University, 1990.

————, with Roger Wade and Loren Weinberg, "Abortion Counseling at the Boulder Valley Clinic," *Frontiers: A Journal of Women's Studies,* Vol. I, No. 2, Spring, 1976.

————, and Roger Wade, *Teenage Abortion Need Not Be a Tragedy.* Educational pamphlet, Boulder, CO, 1978.

Wehr, Demaris S., *Jung and Feminism: Liberating Archetypes.* Boston: Beacon Press, 1987.

Yalom, Irvin, *Existential Psychotherapy.* New York: Basic Books, 1980.

Young-Eisendrath, Polly, and Florence Wiedemann, *Female Authority.* New York: The Guilford Press, 1987.

Zukav, Gary, *The Seat of the Soul.* New York: Fireside (Simon & Schuster), 1990.

NOTES

LIFE, LOVE, MOTHERHOOD, AND POWER

1. Starhawk, *Dreaming the Dark*. Boston: Beacon Press, 1982.

2. Sarah Blaffer Hrdy, *Mother Nature—History of Mothers, Infants, and Natural Selection*, p. 316.

3. Ibid, p. 294.

4. Ibid, p. 470.

5. Ibid, p. 89.

6. Ibid, p. 90.

7. *Conscience: The Magazine of Catholics For A Free Choice*, Nov./Dec. 1989.

8. Hrdy, p. 472.

9. Harold J. Morowitz and James S. Trefill, *The Facts of Life—Science and the Abortion Controversy*.

10. Adrienne Rich, *Of Woman Born*, pp. 281-282.

11. Rickie Solinger, *Beggars and Choosers*, p. 22.

EMPOWERMENT AND PAIN

12. Carol Gilligan, *In A Different Voice*.

13. I am grateful to Terry Beresford for this idea.

14. Barbara Katz Rothman, *The Tentative Pregnancy*.

15. Barbara Ehrenreich, "The Woman Behind the Fetus," *New York Times,* April 28, 1989.

16. Roger Wade, *For Men About Abortion*.

17. Steven Foster with Meredith Little, *The Four Shields: The Initiatory Seasons of Human Nature*, p. 20.

HISTORY AND WOMEN'S LIVES

18. In Native American thought, we are encouraged to take responsibility and prepare the way for the next *seven* generations. For an in depth discussion of this perspective, in particular the political and spiritual philosophy of the Haudenosaunee, also known as the Iroquois Confederacy, read Akwesasne Notes, ed., *Basic Call to Consciousness*. Summertown, TN: Book Publishing Company, 1995. Orig. pub. 1978.

19. Gerda Lerner, *The Creation of Patriarchy*, p. 37. By permission of Oxford University Press, Inc.

20. Rosalind Pollack Petchesky, *Abortion and Woman's Choice: The State, Sexuality, and Reproductive Freedom.*

21. Excerpt from "Violence: The Heart of Maternal Darkness," from *Of Woman Born: Motherhood as Experience and Institution* by Adrienne Rich. Copyright © 1986, 1976 by W. W. Norton & Company, Inc. Used by permission of the author and W. W. Norton & Company, Inc.

22. Mary Beard, *Woman As A Force In History.*

23. Lerner, *The Creation of Patriarchy*, p. 148.

24. Lerner, *The Creation of Patriarchy*, p. 43.

25. Ibid, *The Creation of Patriarchy*, p. 51.

26. Riane Eisler, *The Chalice and the Blade.*

27. Ibid, pp. 88–89.

28. Frederick Engels, *The Origin of the Family, Private Property, and the State.*

29. Petchesky and Gordon both write extensively about this, as does James C. Mohr in *Abortion in America.*

30. Angela Davis, *Women, Race, and Class*, p. 175, 183, and 204.

31. Angela Davis, *Women, Race, and Class*; Rosalind Petchesky, *Abortion and Woman's Choice*; Rickie Solinger, *Beggars and Choosers*, Linda Gordon, *Woman's Body, Woman's Right*; and Sarah Blaffer Hrdy, *Mother Nature.*

32. Linda Gordon, *Woman's Body, Woman's Right*; Nanette Davis, *From Crime to Choice: The Transformation of Abortion in America.*

33. The U.S. Supreme Court, *Roe v Wade.*

34. Nanette Davis, *From Crime To Choice*, pp. 43–44.

35. Linda Gordon, *Woman's Body, Woman's Right*; Barbara Ehrenreich and Deidre English, *For Her Own Good: 150 Years of the Experts Advice to Women.*

36. Kristin Luker, *Abortion and the Politics of Motherhood.*

37. Anonymous personal journal.

38. Ibid.

39. Excerpt from "Anger and Tenderness," from *Of Woman Born: Motherhood as Experience and Institution* by Adrienne Rich. Copyright © 1986, 1976 by W.

W. Norton & Company, Inc. Used by permission of the author and W. W. Norton & Company, Inc.

40. Alan Guttmacher Institute, see statistics at www.guttmacher.org/pubs /fb_induced_abortion.html.

SPIRITUAL PARADOXES

41. Linda Baker, *Soul Contracts.* Patchwork Press, 1998; *Abortion – A Spiritual Approach,* audiocassette.

GRIEF

42. Hillman, James, *The Soul's Code: In Search of Character and Calling.* New York: Warner Books, 1996.

43. Bill Plotkin, *Nature and the Human Soul.* Novato, CA: New World Library, 2008.

SPIRITUAL CHOICES

44. Prior to the seventh century A.D., Catholic confession was made directly to God through prayer. See www.justforcatholics.org/a23.htm.

45. Kay Gardner, *"Changing,"* on *Mooncircles* audiocassette, Urana Records, 1975.

BEYOND ABORTION

46. See Nancy Folbre, *The Invisible Heart: Economics and Family Values.* New York: The New Press, 2001.

47. Amy Shapiro, "Pro-Love" and the Ensoulement Dilemma, *The Journal of Regression Therapy,* vol. VI, no. 1, December 1992.

ABOUT THE AUTHOR

Linda Weber has been a psychotherapist and spiritual counselor for women for forty years, as well as a writer, singer-songwriter, and rites of passage guide. She became an active feminist in 1970, and was one of the country's first abortion counselors. She helped to start a non-profit abortion/women's health clinic in Boulder, Colorado in 1973, where she created and directed the counseling program.

Linda has spent her life studying history, psychology, and spirituality, and how they intersect. She leads individual women and groups out into the wilderness every summer to experience the power of the Earth's teachings. Her work includes the study of dying as a rite of passage.

Linda performed with a women's *a cappella* ensemble for fifteen years. She is the mother of two daughters and the grandmother of five children. She lives in Boulder, Colorado, and her website is earthskycounseling.com.

Sentient Publications, LLC publishes books on cultural creativity, experimental education, transformative spirituality, holistic health, new science, ecology, and other topics, approached from an integral viewpoint. Our authors are intensely interested in exploring the nature of life from fresh perspectives, addressing life's great questions, and fostering the full expression of the human potential. Sentient Publications' books arise from the spirit of inquiry and the richness of the inherent dialogue between writer and reader.

Our Culture Tools series is designed to give social catalyzers and cultural entrepreneurs the essential information, technology, and inspiration to forge a sustainable, creative, and compassionate world.

We are very interested in hearing from our readers. To direct suggestions or comments to us, or to be added to our mailing list, please contact:

SENTIENT PUBLICATIONS, LLC

1113 Spruce Street
Boulder, CO 80302
303-443-2188
contact@sentientpublications.com
www.sentientpublications.com